THINK AND
GROW
DIGITAL

WHAT THE NET GENERATION
NEEDS TO KNOW
TO SURVIVE AND THRIVE
IN ANY ORGANIZATION

JORIS MERKS-BENJAMINSEN

NEW YORK   CHICAGO   SAN FRANCISCO   ATHENS   LONDON
MADRID   MEXICO CITY   MILAN   NEW DELHI
SINGAPORE   SYDNEY   TORONTO

1 2 3 4 5 6 7 8 9 0   DOC/DOC   1 2 0 9 8 7 6 5 4

ISBN   978-0-07-183536-7
MHID   0-07-183536-9

e-ISBN   978-0-07-183537-4
e-MHID   0-07-183537-7

Library of Congress Cataloging-in-Publication Data
Merks-Benjaminsen, Joris.
   Think and grow digital : what the net generation needs to know to survive and thrive in any organization / Joris Merks-Benjaminsen.
      pages cm
   Includes index.
   ISBN 978-0-07-183536-7 (alk. paper) — ISBN 0-07-183536-9 (alk. paper) 1. Career development. 2. Generation Y—Employment. I. Title.
   HF5381.M3987 2015
   650.1—dc23

                                                                2014029149

McGraw-Hill Education books are available at special quantity discounts to use as premiums and sales promotions or for use in corporate training programs. To contact a representative, please visit the Contact Us pages at www.mhprofessional.com.

CONTENTS

PREFACE

This book is for those people who do not just come to work because they get paid to do so. It is for those who really want to make the biggest possible positive difference, which in the long run is the best way to build a flourishing career and substantial income. If you want to make a positive difference, you'll often need to change the way the people around you work. From time to time that will put you at risk, because people often don't want to change their way of working. I know from experience that the most meaningful road sometimes feels like the bumpiest one. The feeling of doing something meaningful, however, is the biggest reward you can get.

I hope my book inspires you to keep choosing meaning over matter, so that you can morph meaning into matter that never existed before. I hope the book helps you build sustainable working relationships with people who think differently from you and with people from all generations so that everyone involved experiences the joy of achieving more than what the sum of separate parts would have been. Finally, I hope that the book helps you find the highest possible alignment between your goals and those of the people around you. I also hope that it encourages you to reinvent yourself time after time so that you can live as much of your life as possible in a flow that feels natural and productive to you. I wish you all the best and hope you'll enjoy reading it!

ACKNOWLEDGMENTS

This book is the product of a full career of cooperation with a wide variety of professionals: colleagues, clients, partners, and friends. I feel that I have learned at least one thing from every professional I have ever worked with. It is through interaction with others that we learn most, and for that I owe gratitude to all the people who have shared their thoughts, questions, objections, doubts, feedback, feelings, support, observations, and more with me over the years.

I would like to express my gratitude and thanks to Paul van Eden, Amy Bloemendaal, Arthur Anglade, Gijs van der Kolk, Donald Merks, Bas Jansen, Taco van Voorst tot Voorst, and Martijn Geerlings for proofreading my manuscript in various stages and for sharing relevant feedback and questions. The content of this book would not be what it is without your input.

A special thanks to my talented mother-in-law, Thera Benjaminsen, for dedicating her time, passion, and persistence to create the expressive illustrations for this book. Above all, I want to thank my wife, Claire Merks-Benjaminsen, for supporting and encouraging me in spite of all the time it took me, talking things over with me, reading the manuscript and assisting in the editing and design process, and helping me get my book published in the United States. It was an exciting journey for all three of us, and what a team we made.

PART I

CHALLENGES AND OPPORTUNITIES

1

TEN REASONS WHY COMPANIES FAIL TO EMBRACE YOUNG TALENT

Attracting and retaining young professional talent has been both a challenge and a priority for many companies and organizations over the past decades. Even so, it is not always easy for talented young professionals to find jobs and build great careers. When economic times are rough, young professionals tend to be the ones who are struck first and hardest: the last who come in tend to be the first to leave if people need to be let go. Even those youngsters who are fortunate enough to keep their jobs don't have an easy time of it. It can be very hard for young professionals to get the promotions they deserve and to find fulfilling career paths. However, I do expect a big shift in the next decade, as companies now need the new generation of professionals more than ever. That is because today's young professionals are generation Y, also called millennials, the generation that grew up with the Internet, *and* because embracing the Internet and all the developments related to it is one of the hardest challenges that companies face nowadays. Companies need "digital thinkers" to guide them through the new digital world. Digital thinkers, however, are almost a different species from earlier generations of professionals and are therefore hard to attract and retain. Let's dive a bit deeper into exactly what digital thinking means and why it is so hard for companies to embrace it.

Digital thinkers can be found in all generations, but because those in generation Y grew up with the Internet, it is their default mode, their natural state. The members of generation Y were born roughly between the early 1980s or the late 1970s, depending on the definition you choose, and the year 2000, and they are often also referred to as millennials. A young Dutch blogger recently published an article about his life as a millennial and described very powerfully the struggles that generation Y faces:

> I struggle to find a place for myself in a world that doesn't seem to be ready yet for the expectations I have of the 21st century. I hope to live in equal or better wealth than my parents. But how? The world is in crisis, the baby boomers made a mess of the world. The money is gone, unemployment rising, two billion people still living in poverty, new rules and laws emerging everywhere and we consume fifty percent more than mother earth can offer us. How can I make a difference in this world?

Having been born on the edge of generation Y myself, I have experienced firsthand how big the gap can be between young professionals' expectations for their working life and what companies offer them. I've struggled to adapt to existing company structures while preserving my fresh young mindset. The fact that I was born on the edge of the old and new generations may have helped me here.

Millennials have talents different from those of earlier generations. The way they look at the world and business is different from the way any other generation of professionals looked at them. This is because they grew up with the Internet from a very early age, many even from the day they were born. Millennials have been shaped by the presence of the Internet and all the influences related to it. Some people even claim that research shows that millennials' brains are different from those of earlier generations, allowing them to do more parallel processing of small pieces of information, but limiting their ability to focus on one task for a sustained period of time. Where older generations can still remember a time without the Internet, to millennials it was just always there. They always had access to all information and all their friends all the time. They can't imagine an era when you had to meet your friends at a clearly specified place and time, and you would not be able to find each other if you failed to keep that exact appointment; hence, they have a much more flexible view of planning and appointments than previous generations. That kind of difference in attitude can create friction when millennials make appointments with older generations, who are likely to expect a more punctual attitude. Not only do millennials process information differently, but their values are also different.

In many articles and books, generation Y is described as being a bit spoiled by being used to getting almost anything they want instantaneously. Generation Y therefore has often been referred to as "generation me." I personally don't believe that this means that millennials are egotistical. I believe they just attribute more value to individuals in general and have different ways of being social.

While older generations struggle to get familiar with the Internet and developments related to it, generation Y cannot imagine a life without it.

The fact that millennials are so different is precisely why they are likely to have to struggle early in their careers. Not only do they face a lack of jobs and growth opportunities, but they are also entering at the bottom of companies created and run by older generations who do not have the same open, flexible, and digital mindset. Hence existing company structures often create an environment that isn't anywhere close to the natural gen Y habitat. Many millennials may therefore experience a culture shock when they try to adapt to office life, and as a result, they may not feel as happy as they could, may fail to perform as well as they could, and may decide to leave the company earlier than necessary. Such a disconnect is a loss not only for these youngsters but also for the companies they work for. Millennials are the new talents that companies need to attract and keep if they are to survive the twenty-first century.

Of course you do not have to be a millennial to be a digital thinker. If you are older than the millennials but you have a more than average interest in the Internet and technology and how they affect people's lives, you are definitely the kind of professional who can help companies be ready for the future. Because of your maturity, you may even be in a great position to help with mobilizing millennials in companies. This book is meant to help all kinds of digital thinkers use their talents to build great careers by helping companies and organizations be future-ready. The majority of all companies are in the process of adapting their strategies in one way or another to get ready for a digital future. So if you are a digital thinker, your mindset is a gold mine, and as I'll show you in the next chapter, CEOs are aware of that fact. You don't have to be a programmer or some other type of IT specialist. Just the fact that you've given the Internet and technology a substantial role in your life makes the things that you see, do, and think extremely valuable for companies. Thus, your digital qualities offer you many opportunities to build a successful career if you learn to use them the right way.

If you are a digital thinker who is part of generation Y, you probably don't relate to the gen Y or millennial label at all. Gen Y doesn't seem to like labels. You might be able to relate to the mindset, though. Here are 10 common mismatches between the millennial lifestyle and the classical nine-to-five office culture as established by generations before you. If you are a millennial, you may recognize them. Individual people, of course, have different experiences, and the likelihood of your bumping into common issues also varies, depending on the type of company (or companies) you work for. For instance, you may bump into different situations when working for small companies as opposed to big ones and the type of manager you have also affect whether you encounter problems and, if so, what type. If you are a millennial, though, at some point in your career, you are likely to run into many of the experiences outlined here. People older than millennials may also bump into similar issues just because they have what you could call an independent mind. I personally bumped into most of them despite my somewhat older age.

1. Why Work Nine to Five, Monday Through Friday?

The most obvious mismatch between office culture and the millennial lifestyle is nine-to-five work life. For millennials, the Internet is always on. They tend to check their e-mail and Facebook first thing in the morning and again before they go to bed. Because the Internet is embedded in almost everything that millennials do, they have developed a very flexible lifestyle, and they work whenever an idea emerges—whether it is at ten o'clock in the morning on a Tuesday or nine at night on a Saturday. The downside to that is that it can sometimes be hard for millennials to know when to switch off work mode. However, those who know how to find that switch at the right moments are likely to be happiest and most productive when they are given the right amount of freedom. Nine to five is a limiting grid. It's limiting for millennials because it means that they can't arrange their lives in the way that works best for them. It's limiting for companies because the inspiration to do something great does not always come between nine and five, so companies lose out on great work and great ideas if they force their employees to work nine to five.

2. Why Work from an Office?

Like the nine-to-five limitation, the office as an obligatory work location does not make sense to gen Y. With e-mail, mobile phones, and video-conferencing always available, this generation does not feel the need to go to the same office every day. Why waste time commuting if you can do almost all aspects of your work at home? The office is still useful, but only as a physical meeting place, a place for conversations and watercooler chats, and a place for coming together every now and then. When going to the office is an obligation, gen Y finds it more limiting than valuable.

3. Why Burden Yourself with Knowledge?

For older generations, having extensive knowledge about a variety of topics and being able to display that knowledge is often an important aspect of building credibility. In an office culture, that credibility can help you get colleagues to listen to your ideas. Hence, spending part of your time displaying the things you know and telling knowledgeable stories during lunch, meetings, or watercooler moments can pay off. Such stories typically display your latest information about, for instance, the news or politics. Gen Y is different. Since information has always been available to these people at a keystroke, they don't see the need to build a huge database of knowledge in their heads. They know where and how to get information instantly when they need it. When older generations spend time proving their worth and knowledge, gen Y sometimes views this as pontification or just a waste of time.

4. Why Have Regular Weekly Group Meetings?

Many companies have weekly meetings where teams come together to prepare for the upcoming week or recap the work done in the past week. These meetings are often repetitive and feel more like a routine than a real necessity. Members of gen Y do not tend to come together in fixed groups at fixed times the way some teams used to. They tailor their meetings to their individual needs at each moment. Because their friends have always been just a click away, millennials have unknowingly acquired the skills to connect to whomever they need at any time. They don't have fixed teams or groups—such a structure can even feel like a waste of time to them. If people need to come together for a project, digital thinkers will know where to find the right people at the right time and bring them together in a conference room, through a chat, by phone, or in a videoconference.

5. Why Is Some Information Limited to *Some* People?

In traditional companies, there tends to be a secretive wall around senior managers' discussions. Junior employees typically learn about important topics only after decisions have been made and are irreversible. This makes many young professionals feel disconnected from the company, since they have grown up with so much transparency. The Internet democratized information, and so millennials feel that everyone has an equal right to information. They need to understand the challenges and opportunities of the companies they work for, and they want to understand how and why those senior to them define strategies to face those issues. If senior managers take more time to share their thoughts and plans at an early stage, they can expect a much more dedicated attitude from young professionals. At the same time, a lack of such sharing leads to a critical attitude and questioning of company policy.

6. Why Follow Orders?

Just as everyone has a right to equal information, in the eyes of gen Y, everyone has an equal right to have an opinion and to have that opinion heard. If a manager gives directions to a millennial, those instructions will generally be perceived more as guidelines than orders. Millennials tend to feel that their opinion on procedures is just as important as that of the managers who dictate those procedures, and so they are likely to ask questions in order to understand why certain directions were given. If managers fail or refuse to give a further explanation, they are unlikely to get support. If a manager forces millennials to carry out a request without any explanation of why this is important, this usually means that credibility is lost, which may result in a valuable person leaving the team at some point in the future. A request is not valid just because it comes from a more senior person. However, if that person can explain the reasoning behind the request and allow for critical assessment, the request is likely to be handled with great responsibility.

7. Why Sacrifice Your Personal Life?

Gen Y has seen older generations work hard, often at the cost of their short-term personal life. Many of them have seen their parents save money for retirement but not receive their pensions because of a fatal illness, or perhaps their parents saw their pensions decrease in value because of deteriorating economic conditions. Therefore, our new young professionals have developed a resistance to sacrificing happiness now for potential happiness many years down the road. Happiness in both work and life deserves "always on" attention. Work should not cannibalize private life structurally, and work itself should offer some kind of fulfillment or pleasure beyond getting paid. This does not mean that millennials are not willing to work hard. They just tend to have different priorities. This is also why they want to be able to critically assess the validity of more senior employees' requests. Millennials prefer working on things that seem valuable and meaningful to them, and tend to do so in a way that does not harm their personal lives structurally.

8. What Is the Purpose?

The transparency of the Internet has brought down many companies that did not serve their clients with integrity. From an early age, those in gen Y have seen the difference between short-term and long-term success. They are unlikely to settle for a job that offers a good salary but does not have a long-term purpose. Many millennials know that the inevitable trade-offs they make may backfire later. If senior managers have a clear vision of how the company creates value for consumers and the world at large, they provide a feeling of purpose that is extremely valuable to gen Y. With this kind of purpose, work can add fulfillment to the personal lives of millennials, and working hard does not feel like a compromise of their happiness.

9. Who Says I Am Too Young?

Gen Y has grown up watching teenage nerds and kids with guitars and a talent for singing become billion-dollar CEOs or celebrities in just a few years' time. To them, age and time are not measures of the potential for success;

that just doesn't make sense. In many companies, some positions or promotions can be acquired only at a certain age or after being with a company for a certain amount of time. While previous generations patiently waited their turn, gen Y professionals are unlikely to do so. They are too aware of what potential is out there, and they are likely to leave the company if they feel that their age is limiting their ability to capitalize on their skills.

10. No Games, Just Business!

Finally, gen Y professionals tend to dislike office politics. Their focus is to do meaningful work—nothing more and nothing less. They generally feel responsible for their work and want to be the critical owners of it. With this attitude, there is no room for political games. Those are likely to be perceived as a waste of time and as harmful to their personal integrity.

The problem is that most traditional companies are led by people who are much older than the millennial generation. In companies that have been around for decades, at least 70 percent of the employees grew up in a different world from gen Y, and typically this 70 percent holds the senior positions. That majority can therefore easily put pressure on the younger generation to adjust to existing ways of working. Their seniority and the fact that they outnumber the young professionals may even make those younger people doubt that their critical perceptions and feelings are justified. Many great new ideas may therefore end up being seen as the naive thoughts of an inexperienced newbie. If you recognize yourself in these situations or perceptions and if you have ever doubted whether your feelings were justified, do not doubt anymore. You may be trying too hard to fit yourself into the existing company structures. Please don't! You will be happier and more successful in the long run if you stick to who you are, for you have been shaped by the dynamics of the new digital world, and that world is exactly what companies need to adjust to. You are a member of a new generation that is stepping into an office environment that developed during different times. You are facing a hard challenge that many people face. If you are a digital thinker who is somewhat older than gen Y, you may be in a good position to help youngsters find their way, keep their digital mindset, and make it valuable for the company.

The friction between traditional office culture and the millennial mindset was nicely illustrated by an anecdote involving Facebook's CEO and founder Mark Zuckerberg. An early version of Mark's business cards became famous because of the iconic way in which he had his job title printed on them: *"I'm CEO, Bitch."*

Mark Zuckerberg's famous business card is a nice illustration of the way in which millennials defy "traditional office culture," where older people tend to be the ones calling the shots.

Many stories and articles have been written about this business card, and it even made its way into the Facebook movie. Some people say that

Mark's action clearly reflects the fact that at that moment in time, he had no idea how big and important his company would one day be and how much responsibility he would one day carry. This small, bold statement says a lot about the millennial mindset: both about the strengths of those in gen Y and about the risks they face. The statement loudly communicates the energy, drive, and ambitions that many millennials have: Who says I'm too young to be a CEO? Who says my ideas can't fly? Who says I need 50 years to establish myself as a professional? I had a great idea, and I made it happen here and now! The statement underlines the value of believing in your ideas, of standing for your ideals, making them happen, and being proud of your accomplishments. It communicates a healthy disregard for the impossible. Older people in senior positions may not always be better or stronger than you, and there is a point where you should not accept a lack of growth opportunities just because of your young age.

Despite the inspirational and humorous aspects of this statement, some people may also perceive it as arrogant. They may feel that it communicates contempt for those who have achieved less or who just have other ways of being valuable to companies or to the world. The statement does not communicate much respect for competitive companies that may be less successful or possibly are even going bankrupt because of bad economic times or for other reasons. It doesn't communicate much thankfulness for the success achieved. I'm pretty sure all these negative interpretations were not intended, but my experience is that people can be very intolerant when you make bold statements, even if your intentions are positive. If young people walk into a company with the best intentions of making a positive difference by saying that things should be done differently, there is always a risk that they will be seen as arrogant young brats who lack respect for the historic achievements they have been given to build upon. This is the challenge that lies in front of all digital thinkers who want to make a difference in the companies they work for or within the companies that are their clients. How can digital thinkers take their fresh mindsets and change things while keeping as many people on board as possible? How do you get your colleagues and clients to change along with you?

To get a deeper understanding of the sensitive balance between driving change and respecting the prior work of others, I will share a personal experience with you. In my early days as an advertising researcher, I used to test many TV commercials to see if they were effective in raising awareness of brands or in supporting sales. It turned out that at least half the ads weren't effective at all, and often that was for a very clear reason: people recognized the ad but couldn't remember what brand it was for, or they just did not understand the message at all. I remember thinking more than once: "Why did they create this ad in the first place? Anyone can see that this is a terrible ad! You don't need research to prove that." Then I discovered that in most cases, the people involved already knew that the ad wasn't strong. They had even known it before they launched the ad. It took a while for me to realize how many companies, teams, and people work on advertising campaigns from the initial idea until the finished product. Seeing that organizational complexity and acknowledging the political implications of having so many stakeholders helped me understand why so many ads tried to communicate too many messages in too little time. Creating an advertisement is not just about having a great idea, but also about making that idea happen, protecting the original creative and strategic insights throughout all stages of development, and not letting those insights die because of compromise or conflict. By the time the ad was finished, so many people had invested their time, effort, and personal credibility in it that stopping the ad or even acknowledging that it was bad was often just not acceptable anymore. That knowledge helped me respect the art of making great ads, and through that understanding I learned to be helpful in the process of creating advertising by using the findings of my research to improve things without pointing a blaming finger at painful mistakes that people were already aware of.

This example shows how delicate the balance is between wanting to change and improve things and respecting the work that people have already done. I had to challenge the quality of the ads in order to get people to improve them. If I didn't achieve that, what use would my research have been? At the same time, I had to make sure that I was not offending anyone unnecessarily. Offended people are mostly not open to making changes based on your recommendations. They may not be open to hearing your opinion at all. People could even have been unjustifiably fired over my research if I hadn't been careful about how I positioned the results.

Organizing teams or a company to do great things requires more than having a great idea and knowing (or thinking you know) how things need to be done. It also involves the skill of finding the right people to make the idea happen and getting people to cooperate in a way that makes the vision come to life. If a product or service created by a company is not optimal, it is very easy to assume that "these fools don't understand what they are doing." It is always good, though, to realize that your starting point in a company is the achievement of all the people who have worked there before you. They overcame obstacles that you may never encounter and thereby made more things possible than was true a few years ago. If you see that, you will understand better why products or projects are not yet at the stage where you imagine they can be. If you enter a new job, make a habit of getting acquainted with the company, the people, and in particular the history of important products and projects: How did they evolve over time? What problems did people bump into? How were those problems overcome? Or why did they lead to failure? What ideas do people have for approaching things better in the future? You might find that many of your ideas are already in some people's minds, which means that you have supporters, and that is even better than coming up with a new idea that no one has had before. Learn to appreciate the work that has been done. Understand the sensitivities: you might be touching a sensitive topic and destroy many years of stakeholder management by shouting out your vision of what can be done better. If you start any new job by connecting with the right people to hear their views and ideas, you'll be much more effective in assessing the exact value of *your* skills and ideas, in positioning them in the organization, and in getting the support of the right people. These people will help prevent you from falling into the same traps that they fell into.

> *It is always good to realize that your starting point in a company is the achievement of all the people who have worked there before you.*

If you want to make a difference in a company, it is not sufficient that you know (or think you know) how things need to be done. You need to connect with people and mobilize them to join a quest that is meaningful for all of you together.

Throughout my career, I've fallen into many of the typical traps that digital thinkers are vulnerable to: I entered new jobs with fresh new ideas while forgetting to appreciate what was already there and failing to acknowledge that people were under a lot of work pressure; thus they were not really hoping that someone would come up with another "great new idea." Often I tried to change too much at the same time, and many times my positive intentions were misunderstood. I have had moments when I was overexcited about big successes, which some people may have perceived as arrogance. However, these traits that sometimes caused problems or misunderstandings were also the qualities that helped me build success and be valuable to my colleagues and clients. Through failure and success, I've learned to strike a better balance between changing my environment and fitting into existing structures, between challenging people's opinions and embracing them. As I did so, my career path became both more successful and more fulfilling. I felt a lot happier working with my colleagues, and I felt connected, appreciated, and respected.

In this book, I share my experiences and learnings with you. I hope they offer you an accelerated learning curve and a smooth ride for your career. The book will help you find the gold that is hidden in your digital mind. It will help you formulate your personal ambitions so that you can match them to the company's goals. You'll get tools to help older generations see what you see so that together you can make the best out of the old and new worlds. With those tools, you'll grow into an unmissable asset, mobilizing your company to be ready for the future, either as an employee or by running your own business. Digital thinkers have a unique offering to companies. If all people could look at the world through your digital-savvy eyes, companies would embrace the Internet much faster. However, that can happen only if people with different mindsets learn to connect with one another in the right way. If you are a millennial or some other type of digital thinker and you can learn to connect to older generations in the right way, you'll never have to worry about your career again. You will be able to win people to support your ideas and systematically create your own jobs: jobs that may not have existed before, but that are tailored to your talents and that bring out the best of what you have.

Keep your fresh ideas and your energy while systematically building your alignment skills, and one day you will write your own CEO business card (if you aspire to be a CEO, that is). The most important goal of this book is to help you find a career path that allows you to do the kind of work you love doing and that helps you achieve the goals you aspire to. You set your own goals, and I would be honored if one day you feel that this book helped you make them reality.

2

CEOs WANT YOUR POWER

S o, the good news is that digital thinkers have a unique offering that can help companies be future-ready and that can be the basis of great, fulfilling roles and careers. Even better news is that CEOs *want* you to step into those roles. They *want* you to develop your powers of cooperation and persuasion to mobilize their companies. Because it is generally hard to mobilize people around an idea, companies are mostly moving more slowly than you'd expect when you look at them from the outside. CEOs know that the world is changing fast, particularly in this digital era; hence they always have a long wish list of things that they want to achieve and improve. However, these things don't move as fast as they would like, so CEOs often need to be patient and diligent over many years to make their ideas for change happen. In the particular case of adapting to all facets of the new digital world, the additional complexity is that you need to be a native digital person to fully understand the true extent to which things have changed. So CEOs know that their companies are lagging in using the full potential of the digital world and want their companies to speed up in becoming digital, yet their wish list of what exactly to change is less precise than it used to be. So the demand is there, but the solution is not fully clear. You are in a unique position to help CEOs find and drive that solution, since you are a native digital person.

> *CEOs know that their companies are lagging in using the full potential of the digital world and want their companies to speed up in becoming digital, yet their wish list of what exactly to change is less precise than it used to be. So the demand is there, but the solution is not fully clear.*

CEOs want you to help in making their companies future-ready.

The fact that CEOs are so conscious that their companies need to embrace digital faster than they are doing was very surprising to me, but I got that information firsthand from CEOs themselves. In my work for

Google, I have had the opportunity to meet with the CEOs of many multi-national companies and hear their views on embedding digital technologies in their company strategies. Before that, I had seen them as old, gray, resistant guys, stuck in their old-fashioned business thinking. And indeed, these CEOs are from an older generation than I am, yet they repeatedly invited me to speak to them about my experiences in digital marketing and about my research on digital consumer behavior. They asked what I thought their companies should do to be more future-ready. They were open to my opinions, even though my experience was far from matching their track records. They weren't a stubborn, old-fashioned bunch after all!

That made me wonder how I had built this image of CEOs being old-fashioned and narrow-minded, and I discovered that it was based on a false interpretation of my experiences in the early years of my career. In earlier job roles, I had worked mostly with middle managers from the same companies. In these meetings, I routinely dealt with negative and defensive attitudes toward digital change. If research showed that my clients needed to invest more heavily in their digital strategy, the same thing happened over and over again: some young people in the room would be very enthusiastic about the study results and would selectively pick out all the high numbers in the study to make an internal case for digital change. These youngsters, of course, were part of the digital department. Then some older folks in the room would attack the study and its method and question its results in general. My conclusion at that point was the older folks were the old-fashioned leaders who did not (want to) see how much the world had changed. That wasn't true, however. None of these people were the leaders of the company. All of them were middle managers, and middle managers are not responsible for the success of the *whole* company, but only for the success of *their own teams*. The results of my research were the fuel for an internal battle between two or more teams that were competing for the same marketing budgets. Since the world was gradually shifting toward digital, those budgets were gradually shifting between the teams, which could even result in people on the older teams getting fired and more people on the younger teams being hired. No wonder these people were so defensive. They were fighting for their own jobs.

You can imagine my surprise when it turned out that the CEOs wanted to hear everything about digital. In a lot of cases, they had invited a whole lineup of speakers to their events, all of them people as young as I was who came from all kinds of areas of digital expertise. I realized that CEOs are the ones responsible for the overall long-term success of the company, and therefore they need to be forward-looking and think as digitally as they can, regardless of their age. What slows down company progress is office politics and in general the fact that it is hard to mobilize large groups of people to walk in one direction, particularly if that direction leads to a new world that is full of uncertainties. If change and uncertainty result in middle managers competing for limited resources, the CEO's focus and vision get lost because people are protecting the needs of the individual departments rather than those of the company as a whole. CEOs are generally aware of these dynamics, but it is not an easy fix. Instead, it is one that takes time—time that could result in the company's losing out to other companies that are moving faster. That is why CEOs know that they need to attract young professionals and all other types of digital thinkers to help them be successful.

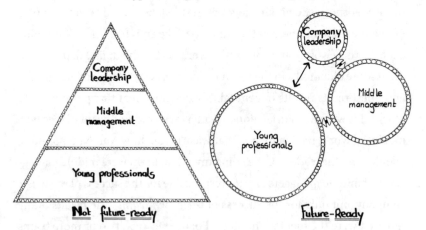

Middle managers can sometimes cause a disconnect between senior managers and the young professionals who are required to help companies become future-ready.

Fixing the 10 problems mentioned in the previous chapter will help today's companies thrive in the future, and you can be sure that CEOs are aware of those problems and are working on making things better. Yet it is hard for CEOs to speak directly to the new generation because there are often many layers of managers in between, and their message often gets lost in translation. If that weren't the case, it would be much easier for young people to find great jobs with great rewards, since digital thinking is the key to surviving in this new digital century.

To fully understand the urgency for companies to adapt to their environment, it is good to be aware of two big trends that are being fueled by the emergence of new technology and the Internet:

1. Increased rate of change
2. Increased transparency

The *increased rate of change* relates to the exponential nature of technical development that was nicely described by the famous Moore's law: Intel cofounder Gordon E. Moore stated that the number of transistors on integrated circuits doubles approximately every two years. Moore described this trend in a 1965 paper. His prediction has proved accurate, in part because the law is now used in the semiconductor industry to guide long-term planning and to set targets for research and development. The capabilities of many digital electronic devices are strongly linked to Moore's law: processing speed, memory capacity, sensors, and even the number and size of pixels in digital cameras. All of these are improving at (roughly) exponential rates, and since technology affects the flow of information, this affects almost any kind of business. It requires organizations to be much more flexible than they were before. A company's flexibility is typically challenged when a change comes along that is so fundamental that it completely transforms the business. Examples are the digitalization of music, books, and photography, and also the emergence of smartphones that can replace a large portion of the digital camera market. Companies that built their business model based on older market dynamics are often late in adopting fundamental new developments. This sometimes happens because the leaders do not see the change coming soon enough, and sometimes it is related to political behavior similar to what I described in my personal experience in presenting research to clients. In the early stages of new developments, the ambassadors of change will be a small group of forward-looking people, people who are eager to learn new things and adapt to new situations. They want to serve consumers and clients utilizing the latest and finest techniques. At the same time, a majority of the people will probably have their roots in "classical knowledge" and in the systems that allowed them to achieve the success they are currently enjoying. If these people do not want to change but also don't want to lose their senior positions, they may start undermining support for the early ambassadors of change in their organizations. They will probably argue that the new developments are cannibalizing the existing business. This is even likely to be true, for fundamentally new developments often cannibalize existing business. However, this is exactly why cannibalization mostly can't be used as a reason for failing to embrace new developments. Doing so makes companies inflexible and resistant to change. The longer that resistance lasts, the longer new young companies have to build their learning curve based on the new technology. This may reach a point where it is no longer possible for the older company to catch up. This can be the end of a company or organization that has been successful for decades. You need the right forward-looking people and a cooperative culture to be at least as dynamic as your changing consumers and clients. If you don't have that, your organization is unlikely to survive this era of accelerating change.

> *You need the right forward-looking people and a cooperative culture to be at least as dynamic as your changing consumers and clients.*

The second trend that is forcing companies to adapt their strategies as fast as possible is the *increased transparency* that comes from consumers and clients having more information than ever and having much more freedom of choice in their purchases. The Internet also offers them a platform for voicing their unhappiness (or happiness) about your service or products. As a result, old-fashioned "polishing" of an intrinsically weak product is a lot less likely to be successful than it was 10 years ago. A strategy of forcing your products on people by having long-lasting self-prolonging contracts or monopoly distribution deals is also less likely to be successful. Sustainable success can no longer be enforced or achieved with shortcuts; it has to be earned. This means that all people in the organization will need to change their mindset to systematically focus on development that will benefit the users or the clients, thereby earning their love for a company's products, services, and brands. If other companies are more successful in achieving that, that knowledge will travel among clients and end users much faster than ever before, which will harm the company's success.

The increased transparency and rate of change amplify each other, putting a lot of pressure on companies to adapt their strategies over and over again. The shortest way to express that is in the following formula:

$$Speed\ of\ change \times transparency = pressure\ to\ adapt$$

The increased speed has made it harder for companies to keep up with all the changes, while the punishment for not keeping up is harder and comes faster because of the new level of transparency. Any employee who can help the company adapt is a highly valuable asset.

When reading this, you may wonder how you can change a big company if you are not formally the leader or even a manager. The good news is that you can lead from anywhere in the organization, even from below. Leadership is not the same as authority. You can even lead people without their noticing that you are leading them, and by that I am *not* referring to manipulation of people. It is about putting forces in place that make the system start moving. That can be done by helping the right people see things that they need to understand, by giving encouragement at the right moments, or by asking the right critical questions. Those are things that millennials can do well. Their digital eyes see things that others don't see, and they were raised to question the information given to them, to challenge opinions, and to ask critical questions.

There is an opportunity for young people to take the (informal) lead. Many managers are used to having people below them who are comfortable with being told what to do. For some people, this gives them a form of direction and security. Our new generation, however, does not really accept that kind of management, as we've seen in the first chapter. Yet it is not always easy for senior managers to adopt a new style of managing. This means that a lot of young people are walking around in companies without fully accepting the existing leaders, even though they have valuable knowledge and skills. The new leadership style is more about support than about control. And giving up control is particularly hard if you have spent years telling people what to do. Hence any digital thinker with leadership qualities and a supportive work style often has the opportunity to motivate people to join a cause. That cause could be your idea for helping the company become future-ready. That person could be you.

There are risks, though, in leading without formal authority, particularly if you fail to connect with people—your colleagues and your direct superiors—in the right way. I'll cover those risks in the next chapter and will also show how you can overcome them if you have the right skills. By sharing knowledge from my conversations with CEOs, I hope to both help you hear their message and give you the tools to have them hear *your* message. That would help in bridging the gap between older and younger people in the organization, and hence will help the company become future-ready. You should not feel the need to adjust to older generations' existing ways of working. You will be hired for your fresh way of thinking and doing things, so make sure you stay fresh and stay who you are. On the other hand, be aware that you cannot do things on your own. This book will help you identify common personalities that you may encounter in your work, so that you can relate to them faster and more easily. That will help you find the best balance, enabling you to listen to other people's opinions without getting trapped in them.

> *By sharing knowledge from my conversations with CEOs, I hope to both help you hear their message and give you the tools to have them hear* your *message.*

THE SUPERHERO DILEMMA

Before we dive into how you can drive change and build your career, let's first delve a bit further into the risks of leading without having formal authority. The dilemma you face is in many ways similar to that of a superhero. Superheroes are simultaneously loved and hated. They are loved because they are incorruptible and can give a strong helping hand to make the world better; they are hated because they are different and can do things that normal people cannot do. Digital thinkers face the same dilemma. Their combination of personality traits gives them the potential to be successful, but that potential goes hand in hand with the risk of being cast aside by other colleagues.

PEOPLE FEAR WHAT THEY CAN'T CONTROL

One trait that can both be a strength and a risk is the nonhierarchical nature of gen Y. While millennials may think that everyone has an equal right to an opinion, others may feel that junior employees should listen to their managers instead of questioning them. They may feel that people who worked for the company longer have earned more right to have their opinions heard. They may see you as competition if you enter a company as a new colleague and start trying to change things right away, especially if you do so successfully. A nonhierarchical mind is harder to control, and

Like superheroes, every generation has its own unique skills, and its members are both loved and feared for the extraordinary things they can do.

some people in general fear whatever they can't control. The art for both young and older digital thinkers is to give people a sense of control by connecting with them, making it clear that you are listening to them, and showing them how your ideas relate to theirs. Try to explicitly show that you took what they told you and embedded it in your thinking and your ways of working. You basically have to make a conscious effort to create a sufficient feeling of being manageable. If you can do that, people will start seeing you as an opportunity rather than a threat. And the truth is, it is very likely that by listening to your managers and your colleagues, you will add a lot of richness to your initial ideas. At the very least, you will find some useful tactics for embedding your work better in the organization, but you may find much more. Many people walk around with great ideas that don't always get heard. If you can find these ideas and help them get heard and happen while giving credit to all the people involved, you'll quickly make friends.

PEOPLE FEAR WHAT THEY CAN'T UNDERSTAND

Another risk is the fact that you may see things that others who did not grow up in the same technological environment as you find hard to grasp. While some people are intrigued by things that they don't understand, others feel threatened by them. My experience, though, is that you can make many people happy if you can help them understand something that they did not expect to grasp before. In a lot of cases, that requires you to explain things that are so obvious to you that you may forget they are largely invisible to others. Place yourself in the position of those who had limited access to the Internet and computers during the first 20 to 50 years of their lives and try to imagine how much new stuff they have to digest in order to understand what you are saying.

I remember telling my grandmother that I had started working for Google. She had no idea what Google was. How do you explain to such a person why Google is so important in this era? This is a question that is completely obvious to most digital thinkers, but if you need to explain the answer to your grandparents, you'll quickly discover how much underlying understanding and knowledge is needed to grasp all the relevant details. You can imagine that more complex topics like social media strategy, digital marketing, cloud-based services, and responsive websites sound like abracadabra even for younger generations than your grandparents. Use the oldest generation around you as a test. If you can explain to people in that generation what you want to achieve, why it is relevant, and how it should be done, you can explain it to anyone. And if you do, you'll see their gratefulness for helping them be more digital-savvy. Don't fall into the trap of throwing around technical buzzwords to sound more intelligent or just because these words have become your natural language. True intelligence lies in being able to help people see what you see (which means that you also need to understand what they see).

Don't fall into the trap of throwing around technical buzzwords to sound more intelligent or just because these words have become your natural language. True intelligence lies in being able to help people see what you see (which means that you also need to understand what they see).

PEOPLE FEAR CHANGE

A third risk lies in the ambition to do great things. If you have great ideas and big plans to make a difference, of course that is a positive thing, but again, not to everyone. As I already mentioned, ambition can be perceived as competitiveness by some people, and there is also a second tricky element to having great ambitions: not everyone wants things to change. People may resist change for many different reasons. They may feel that change means more work, they may fear that they'll need to give things up in order for the change to happen, or they may feel that the change you are proposing is just not feasible. If you walk into people's offices with an idea, someone will almost always say, "We've tried that, but it didn't work." When this happens, you should try to find out why this person thinks your plan will not work. You'll be able to assess how your plan might be or needs to be different from what has been tried before, and thus you'll have the opportunity to address possible objections and get more people on board. In general, there is an art to presenting a lively picture of what the idea can amount to in the final stage while at the same time making the first steps look small and feasible in the short term. Be aware that not everyone is automatically thrilled by big ideas, and make an effort to guide people through your thinking step by step while addressing their potential objections.

Be aware that not everyone is automatically thrilled by big ideas, and make an effort to guide people through your thinking step by step while addressing their potential objections.

PEOPLE MAY FEAR BOTTOM-UP LEADERSHIP

Finally, if you listen to people and make their ideas part of your vision, if you can help them see what you see and get them on board with your projects, you'll be increasingly successful and influential. Though this sounds great, the next risk is that more senior employees may feel that you are undermining their authority by mobilizing groups of people for your personal cause. In fact, they may start feeling that you are undermining the company leadership in general. In the first years of my career, the thought of potentially undermining my superiors never crossed my mind. I always highly respected my superiors and tried to learn as much from them as possible. At the same time, I was not at all aware that my ideas were spreading through the company and that more people had started following them. I had no idea that I was exercising leadership; hence, it did not cross my mind I needed to make sure that my influence on the company was aligned with the plans the company leaders had. When I saw how my influence had grown, I quickly acknowledged that there was no use in undermining the leaders. It wasn't good for me or for the company. People always need some kind of clarity concerning leadership, so the art is finding a way to use your skills to exercise informal leadership and extend the influence of the formal leader. By doing so, you make your skills useful to the senior leaders who are giving the company its direction, and hence you make the biggest positive difference. When you start seeing this, you'll learn to use your influence more consciously. Train yourself to be explicitly transparent to your superiors: explain to them whom you are trying to win for your ideas and why. That way, they'll understand how you are trying to help, and they'll have the opportunity to make you part of their bigger plans for the company.

> *People always need some kind of clarity concerning leadership, so the art is finding a way to use your skills to exercise informal leadership and extend the influence of the formal leader.*

If you do this, you are likely to find that there is a broader context to the things you are working on and that your managers sometimes need to make trade-offs that you may not be aware of. That changes your perspective on the relationship between a manager and a subordinate. Before I realized this, I could look at the relationship as involving either two individuals with equal rights or two organizational positions in different company layers. There is a middle ground in between, though, if you look at a manager and a subordinate as two individuals in different roles with different professional responsibilities. From that angle, it is easier to see how you can help your managers work successfully on their responsibilities while asking them to help you work on yours. This mindset strikes a nice balance between the nonhierarchical millennial mindset and the traditional organizational hierarchy, which also has a useful purpose. Learn to

If you are ambitious and new in a job, it can be tempting to start running immediately, yet if you have some patience and develop the right alignment, you'll mostly work much more effectively.

develop this skill of vertical alignment, for it will help you be more sustainably successful and have a more fulfilling cooperation with your superiors. Be aware, though, that not all managers are ready for open cooperation in which you build a relationship based on mutual support. Some managers are just busy with their own careers or may just think that giving orders is the best way of getting people to do the things they want them to. From person to person, you'll need to assess what is the best way of cooperating. If you are creative, you will always find a way that works for both of you. Later chapters in this book offer guidance on how to relate to various kinds of people you may encounter in your work.

THINK BEFORE YOU RUN

Summing things up, if you are ambitious and entering a new job, it can be very tempting to start running immediately. You may feel that you want to make a difference and want to prove to others that you can do great things and be successful. Jumping into a new job in sprint mode can put you at risk of treading on people's toes, though. Like superheroes, who need to learn to control their powers when they are young to avoid doing damage by accident, ambitious digital thinkers need to learn to hold their breath, connect to people, get the right background information, and start running only when they have the right alignment. You need to be restless and patient at the same time. Like superheroes, you are here to make a difference and to change the world with fresh power, yet you should do so only when the time is right and the necessary steps have been taken so that you can make a powerful start—instead of an uncontrolled crash.

BEWARE OF THE BIG FIVE GEN Y RISKS: ACTIONS TO REMEMBER

1. *Be aware that a nonhierarchical mindset may be interpreted as uncontrollable.* Give people a sense of control by connecting with them, making it clear that you are listening to

them, and showing how your ideas relate to theirs. Explicitly show people how you've embedded their ideas in your plans. Make yourself manageable. Establish a relationship between you and your manager that helps both of you deliver on your responsibilities.

2. *Don't talk in buzzwords or technical terminology.* Step into the footsteps of those who are less familiar with the digital world than you are and help them see what you see. Use those in the oldest generation as a test. If you can explain to them what you want to achieve, why it is relevant, and how it should be done, you can explain it to anyone.

3. *Be aware that not everyone is automatically thrilled by big ideas and change.* Balance your big inspirational ideas with small and feasible short-term steps. Patiently guide people through your thinking step by step while addressing their potential objections.

4. *Beware that you don't create a feeling that you are undermining the company's leaders by driving change within the company.* Be transparent to those who are senior to you whom you are trying to win for your ideas and why. Show how your ideas contribute to your superiors' strategy, and help the company benefit from your ideas and influence.

5. *Don't start running and treading on people's toes the minute you are in a new job.* Use the first weeks in a new job to connect to people and get the right background information, and start running only when you have the right alignment.

PART II

HIT THE
GROUND RUNNING

4

BE ONE WITH YOUR COMPANY

Making a difference in business takes a lot of energy. You get that energy from doing things that give you a feeling of purpose, yet those things need to be relevant for the company you work for as well. This chapter helps you build awareness, both internally and externally.

Internal awareness is all about knowing yourself, what qualities you have, what you like and don't like, and the direction in which you would like to develop. External awareness is about understanding the people, the jobs, and the companies around you (including the company that you work for now), knowing the kinds of jobs that are available, and knowing what will be expected from you. The right combination of internal and external awareness helps you formulate goals for yourself that are in full alignment with your environment. These aligned goals help you keep up your momentum in achieving your ambitions, and they help guard your feeling of purpose throughout your career.

INTERNAL AWARENESS: KNOWING YOURSELF

Awareness is the starting point for building a fulfilling and successful career. Being aware starts with asking yourself some fundamental questions about who you are and why you want to work for a certain company and in a certain job. If you cannot answer these questions, there will be a lack of focus in everything you do, and you are probably not utilizing your talents as well as you could, which again lowers the likelihood of your being sustainably happy and successful in your professional life.

At the start of your career, it can be hard for you to know what you want to be as a professional, what kind of companies you could work for, and what kind of jobs they can offer. Hence, it can be very hard to give your career a meaningful direction. When you are looking at job sites, if you do not have the right knowledge, it is almost impossible for you to assess which jobs have the most potential to fit your skills and to make you happy. A great exercise to get you started in looking for a suitable job is called "Circles of Awareness." I did a similar exercise myself at the start of my career after reading the book *What Color Is Your Parachute?* by Richard Bolles. I found the exercise really useful, and I have used it at various stages of my career and adapted it over time to make it even more useful for me. The Circles of Awareness exercise is one in which you list your skills and interests

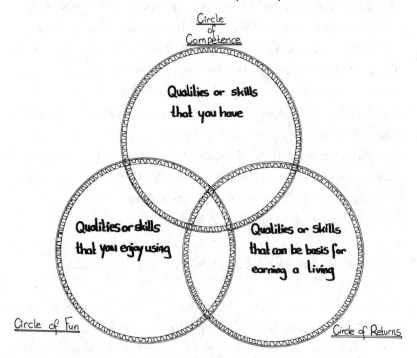

Circles of Awareness: The qualities and skills that you have, that you enjoy using, and that have the potential to earn you a living are the ones that you can build your career on.

and determine which of them are relevant in business. The next step is to start talking to people who you think have interesting jobs. I will give guidance on how you can take the outcome of the exercise along with you and have interesting and useful conversations. Let's start with the exercise first.

EXERCISE

Take a blank sheet of paper and draw three circles. Each circle will represent one of the following Circles of Awareness:

- The Circle of Competence
- The Circle of Fun
- The Circle of Returns

In each of those circles, you can make a list of personal and professional qualities that relate to you as a person. Let's take a deeper look at these circles.

THE CIRCLES OF AWARENESS

The Circle of Competence: Qualities or Skills That You Have

In the Circle of Competence, list all the qualities or skills that you have. Try to be as extensive as possible, and include both concrete and soft skills. A concrete skill could be playing music or working with numbers, while a soft skill could be seeing through people or making people feel welcome. Think about situations in which you have felt a sense of accomplishment, situations in which someone complimented you for doing something well, or situations in which you felt that people reacted positively to something you did. These can be situations in either your professional or your personal life.

In those situations, which skills did you use? Write all of them down. Ask some friends you trust what personal and professional qualities they see in you. Don't forget to think of the digital skills and mindset that you have as a result of growing up with the Internet. The things that you see and can do may not sound unique to you because so many people your age have the same skills; however, as we discussed, your digital experience is extensive compared to that of many people who are in today's workforce. For instance, it may not sound special to you that you can build and maintain communities on Facebook or that you can run a YouTube video channel. However, young people who successfully run social media platforms with millions of followers or subscribers serve as an example for many big companies in defining their digital strategies. Make sure you have included your relevant digital skills in your list.

Once you feel the list is exhaustive, underline the ones that you feel are distinctive. These could be skills that many people have but that are particularly strong in you; or you could have a rare *combination* of skills. In my case, my skill at working with numbers is developed to an extent that could qualify me for jobs that involve number crunching. That skill, however, becomes even more valuable when I connect it to the fact that I can easily relate to all kinds of human emotions. There are a lot of people with number skills, but there are a lot fewer number crunchers who can also easily relate to human emotion. In addition, there are many people who are skilled in working with human emotion, but not so many of them are good with numbers. It is the combination of these two skills that made me suitable as a researcher in the area of advertising and brands, since work in that field requires you to translate numbers into human emotions and vice versa. Another example of a skill that I have is that I am able to present information to audiences in a clear and convincing manner. By adding this to my ability to deal with numbers and human emotions, I have found the exact combination of skills that sets me apart as a professional.

Try to find a set of skills that gives you a fingerprint that is at least somewhat unique while being broad enough to find a match to various kinds of jobs. To help you get started on your list of personal qualities, consider taking an online test that will generate a list of some of your particular personal and professional qualities. One great test is Strengthsfinder 2.0, based on the book by Tom Rath. This test not only gives you a list of qualities, but also generates a list of the types of professional roles that could fit your qualities. Use tools of this kind to create your list, and you will see that you possess more distinctive skills than you knew.

Try to find a set of skills that gives you a fingerprint that is at least somewhat unique while being broad enough to find a match to various kinds of jobs.

The Circle of Fun: Qualities or Skills That You Enjoy Using

In the Circle of Fun, you should list the qualities or skills that you *enjoy* using. These are the skills that give you energy rather than drain it. If you find it hard to identify skills that you enjoy using, try to monitor throughout the day when you feel small uplifts of energy and when you feel your energy drain.

A good exercise that can help you do this is what one of my colleagues calls "the diary of awesomeness." This is an exercise that you can do for a few weeks: at the end of each day (or during the day), list at least three things that you liked about that day. It doesn't matter how small those things are. It could be a moment when you helped a colleague solve a small problem or a moment when you sat down alone to work on some idea that you had. It could be a moment of feeling good after a coffee chat with a colleague. For each of those moments, reflect. What made you feel good at this moment? Why did this moment give you an uplift in energy? What skill(s) were you using? What topic of interest did the moment relate to?

The skills that you enjoy using are not necessarily the ones that you have, and the skills that you have are not necessarily the ones that you enjoy using. In my personal case, for instance, I am good with numbers, but if I do too much number crunching, I start to feel numb because I miss the human aspect. As a student, I started studying physics because I happened to be good at it, but despite having good grades, I didn't feel very happy taking the class. I switched to science of communication and, within that, kept a quantitative angle. At that point, I had no idea what that meant for the potential direction of my career; I just felt happier doing it. However, I eventually came to realize that this subject fit perfectly with my development toward becoming an advertising and brand researcher and strategist later in my life.

> *The skills that you enjoy using are not necessarily the ones that you have, and the skills that you have are not necessarily the ones that you enjoy using.*

Once you have a list of qualities that you enjoy using, do a final check by visualizing how much you would still enjoy using them if you used them every day over many years. There are many skills that are nice to use as long as you don't use them too often. I can feel happy doing quantitative analysis on occasion. It is only when I do nothing other than that for several months that it starts draining my energy. Similarly, many people enjoy dancing every now and then, but would they still enjoy it if they had to do it every day for eight hours a day? Most of them probably would not, so it's better not to make a profession out of it in that case.

The Circle of Returns: Qualities and Skills That Can Be a Basis for Earning You a Living

Finally, in the Circle of Returns, list the qualities or skills that you think are relevant to companies or that would allow you to earn some kind of living in a sustainable way. Sustainability relates to the extent to which you feel you can keep developing those qualities over time and the extent to which they are likely to stay relevant in delivering your income. One thing that helps keep skills relevant is if they are transferrable between jobs and toward the future.

> *One thing that helps keep skills relevant is if they are transferrable between jobs and toward the future.*

My wife was a professional ballet dancer from a very early age through her twenties. Toward the end of her ballet career, she wanted to go in a different direction, but her ballet skills were not transferable to office jobs. She had to completely redo her education, and she became a digital planner for a media agency. That kind of switch takes a lot of time and effort. In her early thirties, my wife had to completely restart her career.

The fact that she changed careers doesn't mean that her ballet career was a negative decision; however, this kind of career choice should be made very consciously. You can imagine that making a conscious choice is hard when you are a child of 12 or younger, which is generally the age when people have to choose whether or not to pursue a professional career in ballet. After that, the body is generally no longer capable of adapting sufficiently to meet the requirements for achieving a professional level in ballet. For most people, though, the really hard trade-offs come at a later stage of their lives, and most young adults are capable of making conscious trade-offs when they are choosing what skills to develop and what passions to pursue. Luckily, on top of that, pursuing a passion doesn't always need to conflict with earning a good living, and a lot of skills that come from following your passion are transferable in many ways. If you do it right, earning a good living can even help you focus *more* on your passions. If you chase a passion that is unlikely to deliver you a sustainable income, you'll probably need a job in addition to your passion to earn your living, which will always diminish the amount of time that you can spend on your passion. So it always pays to think about ways of combining the things you care about with making money off them. I had already discovered at a young age that I was good at acquiring new skills and then helping others to acquire them as well. Therefore, my first thought when it came to my career was becoming a teacher. I realized, though, that teachers don't make a lot of money, and furthermore, if you start as a teacher, you most likely will still be a teacher 40 years later. This is OK if being a teacher is your big passion. However, I saw many more ways of utilizing my talent for acquiring skills and sharing them with others. For example, presenting research results to clients has many similarities to being a teacher; however, this way of using my talents gives me much more flexibility in building my career. More recently, my role started to move away from research because at some point I had seen so many studies and had been in so many conversations with clients that the knowledge base in my head had started to gain value even without the availability of research and numbers. I now present about brand strategy, changes in the digital landscape, and how these things affect marketing, advertising, and brand management. This use of my talents is still related to teaching, yet the topic has broadened, which means that it is sustainably interesting for me and that the financial value of what I do even increases over time. I can still imagine changing my career to teaching or coaching, but I currently still see a path working in marketing and advertising and helping companies grow digital. Any experience I gain now will only make me a stronger teacher or coach later if I decide to make the switch.

My view here is pretty simple: you've got to make a living somehow, and it is nice to spend as much time as possible doing things that you care about, so why not combine the two? This makes you both better at your profession and happier as a person. With these thoughts in mind, list those qualities that you think have some kind of commercial value and that offer you a career path that can keep developing in your desired direction over time.

The Funnel of Focus: Getting from Personal Qualities to Jobs

If you find it difficult to list the qualities that you have, or if later in the exercise it turns out to be hard to match your qualities to specific jobs, there is a great and useful tool that we often use in various kinds of brainstorming at Google; that tool is called the Funnel of Focus.

The Funnel of Focus helps you expand your thoughts if you started with a quality that is so narrow that it may not translate into multiple jobs. It also helps you narrow down your thoughts if you started with a quality that is so generic that it doesn't give you any guidance when it comes to thinking about what jobs are related to it. The narrowest quality would be that you are good at a specific task, such as drawing, a specific sport, presenting, or teaching. A specific *task* that you are good at can be a great starting point if you find it hard to assess your generic qualities. You can extend from the task to the *skills* that enable you to perform that task by asking: "Why is it that I am good at . . . ?"

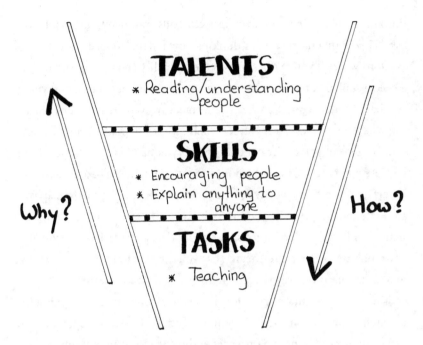

If you find it hard to list your qualities or to match your qualities to possible jobs, use the Funnel of Focus to expand your qualities or narrow them down.

If you are good at teaching, you might find that you can do that well because you can explain anything to anyone or because you are good at encouraging people to discover new things. You can now start thinking about other kinds of jobs where you could also use those skills. If you still feel that your skills are too narrow to be good anchors for thought, you can ask again: "Why is it that I am good at . . . ?" It might be that you are good at explaining things and encouraging people because you have a *talent* for understanding and reading people. You should then think about what kinds of jobs require the skills of understanding and reading people. The process also works the other way around. If you find that you have a talent for understanding people, you can make that more concrete by asking: "How do I know that I have a talent for . . . ?" This question makes you think about how you got to the conclusion that you have a certain talent. It makes you look for the concrete points, which are the underlying skills that you have and tasks that you can do well. If you ask, "Why?," it expands your thinking, which brings you from tasks to skills and then to talents. If you ask, "How?," that narrows your thinking down in the opposite direction.

Don't worry if you're not sure whether a quality you've come up with is a task, a skill, or a talent. Just put it where you think it fits best and you'll see that it works no matter what. For instance, you could argue that teaching is a talent, not a skill. If you see teaching as a talent, the "How?" question could lead you to the conclusion that you have a talent for teaching because you have the skill of reading and understanding people, and that is perfectly fine. The objective of the tool is not to be right, but to help you generate meaningful qualities in each circle so that you have input that helps you find a variety of jobs that could be a potential fit for you and your ambitions. That also means that you are free to mix talents, skills, and tasks when you are listing them in your Circles of Awareness.

There is one additional thing to be aware of when you are looking for a match between your qualities and potential jobs. A single type of job can be totally different in nature, depending on the company you choose. For instance, "account manager" is one of those job titles that is used a lot, but that can have a totally different meaning in different companies. If you work for a highly commercially driven company, the job tends to be closer to that of a salesperson bringing in new clients. However, this same job in another company can involve looking after existing client relationships. The nature of a job also varies, depending on the size of the company. Bigger companies tend to have clearer processes and responsibilities. The advantage of that is that you can learn from other people's experience. The disadvantage is that your job might involve a very narrow area of responsibility. On the other hand, working at a big company also means that you tend to have more opportunities for growth if you are a specialist in a narrow field. If you work for a small or start-up company, there is always an opportunity to pick up a broad range of tasks that in bigger companies would already be owned by other people. So, in a small company, you are more likely to build broad experience. The disadvantage of this kind of company is that there are most likely fewer senior people to learn from, which means that you often have to use your own best judgment to find out how to do things.

A single type of job can be totally different in nature, depending on the company you choose.

If you've started your career working for smaller companies or start-ups, you may find yourself longing to see firsthand how bigger and more experienced companies do the things that you do. A switch to a bigger company could satisfy that longing, but there are also other ways to get the same information. There is a lot of value, for instance, in building a network of similar professionals working for different types of companies. In such a network, you can exchange information about your experiences and see how people approach similar work in different circumstances. Exchanges of knowledge and experience in such a network can accelerate your growth curve and help you clarify what kind of company you'd like to work at next. And of course, once you know where you'd like to work, the people in that same network might be able to help you actually get that job by connecting you to the right people and recommending you. There is no right or wrong in the decision to work for either a small or a big company. You'll need to assess what fits your ambitions, personality, and situation best. I personally have chosen a mix. I have worked in companies varying in size from four, to fifty, to a hundred and even thousands of people. I got something different out of every experience, and each had its pros and cons.

Now, look at your lists of qualities and see which of the qualities are in each of the three Circles of Awareness. These are the qualities that form a good starting point for defining the kind of career or job that suits you best. If you don't immediately see how the qualities can create a full career, don't worry. Just start with the job you want now. If that job is based on a conscious evaluation of the skills that you have, that you love using, and that can earn you a sustainable living, it is likely to be a meaningful choice as part of your overall career path.

If that job is based on a conscious evaluation of the skills that you have, that you love using, and that can earn you a sustainable living, it is likely to be a meaningful choice as part of your overall career path.

Looking at the qualities that are in all three circles, ask yourself following questions:

1. What are the kinds of jobs where I could use and/or develop these qualities?
2. What are the kinds of companies where I could use and/or develop these qualities?
3. What kind of people do I know that work for such companies or in similar jobs?
4. If you aim to start your own business, what would be the kind of business where these skills would add most value for potential clients?
5. Which people do I know who run a similar business?

Maybe you don't directly know people who work in the right jobs, but you are likely to know people who know the right people and are willing to connect you to them. Ask around in your personal and professional networks. Talk to people about the kind of skills you feel you have and how you think you can use them. Ask them for feedback; you may have overlooked valuable skills that they see in you, or you may have overstated some of your skills. Start with people who are close to you to practice. Those conversations will help you gain even more clarity concerning what you are capable of and how you can utilize it. Then, gradually shift to people who may be further from your personal circle of friends. In every conversation, make sure you finish with the question: "Do you know anyone who may be able to tell me more about this kind of job?" That doesn't necessarily mean that those people actually *have* a job for you, but it will gradually bring you closer to it.

Try not to focus too much on *finding* the job. Focus on learning about various job types and which ones are the best fit with your skills and ambitions. If you do that, the conversations will be more enjoyable, both for you and for the person you are talking to. A lot of people enjoy talking about their passions, what makes their job nice, and in what direction they would like to develop. Ask people what they are working on, what their career path looked like, how they got to their current job, what they like about it, what they don't like about it, and how they made their career choices. If you have enough of these conversations, you'll become more conscious of what you want, and you'll get lots of referrals with varying potential. If you focus on connecting sincerely with each individual person in front of you, speaking openly about your passions and ambitions, at some point you will bump into the job you want. It is inevitable that you will do so; it is just a matter of time.

EXTERNAL AWARENESS: CREATE OBJECTIVES IN ALIGNMENT WITH YOUR ENVIRONMENT

If you have had enough conversations with the right people, you will be at the point where you either are considering a new job or have already taken one. If so, it is time to take the next step in the awareness exercise. Try to translate the skills you want to use and develop into long- and short-term objectives and align those with the company you work for now or the company that you may want to work for in the future. If you do this exercise for your existing job, you'll seek alignment with your colleagues and your superiors to ensure that they all agree that you are working on the right things. If you are thinking about a potential new job, you can first define your own objectives and then try to match those with the company during job interviews. This will help you paint a detailed picture of what the job will look like and whether or not it is a good match. If you aim to start your own business, these objectives could be part of your business plan. A good framework for formulating objectives is given here:

- *Short-term objectives.* This involves the alignment of actions and/or concrete projects on a quarterly basis. Define the projects that you think are relevant in the upcoming three months and match them to what is expected from you.
- *Medium-term objectives.* This involves the alignment of topics and goals for the upcoming year. Define and agree with the company on which topics should be given priority over others and how that translates into your goals for the year.

- *Long-term objectives*. This involves the alignment of your wishes for development with those of the company. Define which skills you want to develop and in which direction you hope your role develops, and check how that matches with where the company is moving, what is expected of you, and how the company is willing to invest in you.

- *Lifetime objectives*. This involves the alignment of your ideas about company culture and ethical standards with those of the company. Who do you want to be as a person? In what atmosphere do you want to work? What do you want to bring to the world or to your professional field? If you (plan to) work for a company: How do senior leaders in the company view the field of work you are in? How do they want to provide value to clients and customers? How well do they define their strategies to execute on that? How do they view company culture? How does that match your objectives and ethical standards?

If you complete your awareness exercise by translating your ambitions into objectives on these four levels, you'll discover at the earliest possible stage whether you are still on the right track or not. It is very normal for a certain job or company to have a meaningful place in your career only within a certain period of time. Very few people nowadays spend their whole careers working within one company. A job can be a temporary but meaningful stepping-stone even if you are only in the job for a couple of years. You might, for instance, take a certain job because you know that you can develop skills that you want to utilize later in your career, whether you are aiming to work for a company that you admire, work for yourself as a freelancer, or start your own business.

> *A job can be a temporary but meaningful stepping-stone even if you are only in the job for a couple of years.*

In the early years of my career, I worked as an account executive for an advertising agency. I remember that at that point, I admired the company's brand strategist and talked to him about how he got into that role.

It became clear to me that strategists are rarely people who have worked in an advertising agency their whole lives. They mostly crossed over from marketing roles, media roles, or research roles. This made me decide to switch to advertising research, where I developed myself into a consultant on brand strategy and advertising effectiveness. Later on, in a similar fashion, I decided to make a crossover that would allow me to dive more deeply into the digital aspects of marketing, advertising, and building brands, which brought me to my current job at Google. It is easier to bring out the maximum potential of a job if you are conscious of the part that the job plays in the bigger scheme of things. It will also be easier for you to accept the limitations of the job if you know that you will move on after a few years.

The first two of the four objective levels are somewhat operational in nature and generally require that you have a conversation with your manager and other stakeholders about how you can create the most value for the company given your skill set, your role, and the support you need to make things happen. There is opportunity here for you to shape your job to provide what you want to get out of it, if you can convince others that how you see yourself can add value. To do this effectively, you need to know both yourself and the company well. The better you understand the company's objectives and strategies and your own strengths and weaknesses, the better you will be able to shape your job to accommodate both yourself and the company. It may sound selfish to try to shape your job to match your personal needs, yet doing so is also beneficial to your company if you do it right. First of all, you help the company use the particular skills that you have and that you enjoy using. Using these skills means that you will put more energy into the job and will be more successful. Second, you create a career path for yourself that allows you to stay with the company as long as possible, which means that your employer benefits from you longer. In Chapter 8, "The Job-Creation Formula," I share best practices in shaping and creating your own tailored jobs.

It may sound selfish to try to shape your job to match your personal needs, yet doing so is also beneficial to your company if you do it right.

The alignment of long-term and lifetime objectives can be considered a growth process. This is not something that you do overnight. As you progress in your career, you will gradually learn more about yourself; about your professional values, your strengths, and your weaknesses; and about the situations in which you perform best. At the same time, it takes time to understand the deeper objectives and intentions of the company's senior management. A strategy of trial and reflection often works best here. You can start working based on some initial "light" alignment of short- and medium-term goals. Meanwhile, invest some of your time in getting to know and understand the company better. Every once in a while, you should also take the time to reflect on how you feel about your job. By periodically matching these two and having conversations about those subjects with stakeholders or a coach, you can create the right match between long-term and lifetime objectives and assess whether you are still working for the right company and in the right job.

FINDING PURPOSE IN YOUR JOB AND KEEPING MOMENTUM

If you manage to find full alignment between your strengths, ambitions, and values and those of the job and the company, you are in a lucky space. You will be working on things that you personally care about, and hence you will have a feeling of purpose. The word *purpose* is often used in the context of doing charitable things for the world. I believe, however, that it is more than that. Not everyone can have a world- or lifesaving job, but I believe everyone can experience purpose in their job.

> *Not everyone can have a world- or lifesaving job, but I believe everyone can experience purpose in their job.*

Purpose is a personal thing; you can define for yourself what you feel is meaningful about your job. In my case, you could say that working in marketing and advertising is similar to selling people things that they don't need. If you put it like that, jobs in the area of marketing and advertising are highly unlikely to give you any feeling of purpose. However, I feel that my job helps me educate businesses on changing consumer behavior and business strategies. By doing so, I help people in those businesses to be more successful and happier in their jobs, and I help them build more relevant products and services that are in tune with the twenty-first-century digital lifestyle.

By choosing how you define your job, you can create your own purpose. A clear definition of what purpose means to you in your particular job helps you in prioritizing what parts of your job to develop and pay attention to. It shapes how you perform tasks in your job, and thereby helps you attract more tasks that give you a feeling of purpose. I believe anyone can do this, at least to some extent.

A feeling of purpose makes everything you do convincing and powerful. You will build successes without focusing on promotions and salary. You will achieve your targets just by doing what you feel is right. You'll perform better under pressure and in circumstances that are ambiguous. Purpose provides both perseverance and direction. A nice bonus there: if you structurally reach your targets, you will have more freedom to define your job the way you want to define it, since you will have proved that your method works. When you are working with colleagues, your sense of purpose puts you in a position to help them achieve their objectives because you *want* to help them, not because you *have* to. And rest assured, they will notice the difference and be grateful for it. You will work with a mindset that is impossible to fake by someone who is just there to make money. It is like having the X factor, or a spark that is missing in others who do not feel the same purpose in what they do. You will start any topic by being a lover of the subject, and because of that, you will invest more time and effort than others in becoming a master of it.

A feeling of purpose makes everything you do convincing and powerful. You will build successes without focusing on promotions and salary.

The concept of being a *lover* versus being a *master* of the subject is a powerful one to plan your career with. A master of the subject is someone who has investigated all possible angles of the topic and whom you can generally ask any question about the matter and get a meaningful answer. That doesn't necessarily mean that the master knows everything. Part of being a master is knowing the limitations of your knowledge. A master of the subject tends to be happy to receive a question she doesn't know the answer to, since it challenges her to rethink and improve things that she already knows. The subject you are master of can be as narrow or as broad as you want it to be. It is up to you to draw the circle that defines your area of competence and responsibility.

> *A master of the subject tends to be happy to receive a question she doesn't know the answer to, since it challenges her to rethink and improve things that she already knows.*

Within that circle, make sure that you deliver perfect quality. You can extend that circle over time, depending on what you believe you can handle. I still remember my first client meeting when I was working at the advertising agency at the beginning of my career. I was very nervous, and I wasn't sure what value I could add in the meeting. Then, at some point during the meeting, a question about the project planning came up—a simple question about when certain materials needed to be finished. I was able to pull out the planning that I had done and identify the required delivery date. That made me the expert on project planning in that small moment in time, and my manager was kind enough to compliment me for being on top of that. From that moment on, I made sure that I always had the full project plan in my head. I took ownership of it, and people knew that they could come to me to ask questions about it. You can define what you want to be a master of based on what you care about, what skills you have, and what you think matters to the company. As your career progresses, your mastery will get broader and deeper.

Once you are a master of a subject, try to actively search for new topics that intrigue you. You will again start as a lover of the subject. This time, however, you bring along the master skills that you acquired before, so you will be even stronger than before.

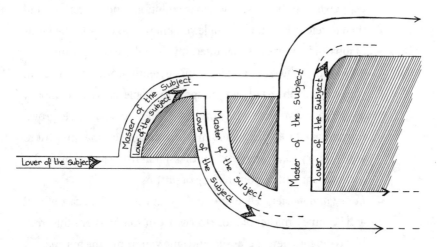

Focus on skills and topics that you love and become a master of them, then extend your work and skills to new topics that you feel passionate about and can master.

Try to find that place in your career where as many elements as possible are aligned: where you have the opportunity to work on things that you love and become a master of skills that are valuable to you. If you already have that, be grateful and express that gratefulness by building on it. If you can keep that momentum of building master skills based on topics you love and time after time can find new topics you love to build new master skills upon, you will have a beautiful and fulfilling career ahead of you!

> Try to find that place in your career where as many elements as possible are aligned: where you have the opportunity to work on things that you love and become a master of skills that are valuable to you.

ACTIONS TO REMEMBER

- *Internal awareness.* Complete the exercise, plotting your qualities in each of the three circles. Identify which qualities can be found in each circle. Identify the kinds of jobs and companies that would allow you to utilize those qualities.

- *External awareness.* Formulate short-term, medium-term, long-term, and lifetime objectives for your career. Start talking to relevant people, first to friends about your ambitions and reflections and then to referrals or other people you know who work in the kinds of jobs and companies that interest you. If there is opportunity to grow within the company that you currently work for or even in your current job, make sure you speak to people inside the company as well so that you can create the room you need if you are to grow.
- *Purpose.* Define which elements of your job are meaningful to you, and try to arrange your professional life around those elements to maximize your feeling of purpose.
- *Lovers and masters.* Dive into topics that you love and care about, and become a master of those topics. Keep your master skills fresh by diving into new topics that intrigue you from time to time.

If you experience problems formulating skills or objectives in your awareness exercise, or in listing things that give you a feeling of purpose, just write something down for now. You can revise what you wrote down an endless number of times as you speak to more people about your goals and as your career progresses over the years. There is no need to have a 100 percent perfect plan now.

CHOICES IN A WORLD OF
ENDLESS OPTIONS

After you have aligned your aspirations and talents with the company's goals and set your objectives, the big challenge is *sticking* to those objectives. It is too easy to be lured into the daily rat race by agreeing to every short-term request. People of all kinds might want things from you that may or may not be in line with your goals. On the one hand, you don't want to be inflexible and unhelpful, but on the other hand, you need to stay focused if you want to succeed and keep your career plan going. The goals and priorities that you determined in the previous chapter will help you decide which requests are aligned with your skills and objectives and which requests you would be better off saying no to. This chapter goes on to show how clear objectives help you filter noise faster and help you stay focused so that you can make progress on the things that matter most to you.

Depending on your profession, there will always be a continuous flow of small short-term tasks. Keeping your e-mail inbox empty is probably the most common small task that always feels urgent but can consume more time than you think. It is very easy to have your whole working day consumed by e-mails that come in; each of them takes no more than five or ten minutes to answer, yet together they may take up all or most of your time. If you give in to always answering each e-mail as it comes

People will always come at you with big or small requests that from their perspective will always be reasonable. You are the only one who oversees your total workload, so you are the only one who can decide whether or not you have room for another task on top of your to-do list.

in, this may, for example, block you from sitting down for a few hours to write that big article you wanted to publish, to create that new client proposal, or to draft a new idea that has been buzzing in your head for a while. And often it is not just e-mails that are coming in, but also the phone is ringing and people are stopping by your desk to make small requests or just to chitchat. The difficulty lies in the fact that all the tasks mentioned, including socializing with your colleagues, are important to some extent. If all tasks are important to the company in some way, then how will you prioritize what to do and what not to do at any given moment? How do you make sure that you are always working on the right things and that your colleagues acknowledge that fact?

One core element of the problem is the fact that there tends to be a tension between short-term urgency and long-term relevance. Tasks that make a big difference in the long term tend to be the ones that feel less urgent in the short term and that also require you to focus for a sustained period of time without disturbance. A commonly used and useful tool to check whether you have the right balance between long- and short-term goals is the urgency/importance matrix. On the vertical axis of this matrix, you plot more important versus less important tasks, and on the horizontal axis, you plot tasks that feel more urgent versus tasks that feel less urgent. As a result, you've created four categories into which you can group the things you do. The matrix actually works both for your personal and your work life.

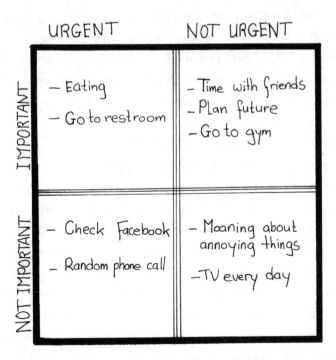

Use the urgency/importance matrix from time to time to check whether you are still working on the right things.

One core element of the problem is the fact that there tends to be a tension between short-term urgency and long-term relevance.

The easiest cell of the matrix to deal with is the cell "not important and not urgent": these are things that you should not allow to take too much time away from the other cells. Casual examples for this cell could be watching TV every night or spending too much time complaining about things that you can't change. The other easy cell is the "urgent and important" cell. These are the things that automatically will demand your attention and that you are always justified spending your time on. Casual examples there would be eating and going to the toilet. The hard thing is striking the right balance between the "urgent but not important" and "important but not urgent" cells. Casual examples for "urgent but not important" would be, for instance, answering a phone call or checking each Facebook message as soon as it comes in. Casual examples for "important but not urgent" would be spending time with friends, planning your future, and exercising regularly. Many people who do this urgency-versus-importance exercise for their work discover that they spend far too much time working on many small things that seem urgent now but that are actually less important than some other tasks that have longer-term importance; those other tasks don't force you to pay attention to them in the short term.

At work, the regular daily tasks like answering e-mails, phone calls, and small requests by all kinds of people around you are generally the ones that tend to feel urgent in the short term and that seem to have quick fixes that will take very little of your time. The problem is just that there are so many of these tasks. For many professionals, this is a flow that never stops if you don't make an active effort to give priority to other things. Many professionals feel that they are doing all kinds of small stuff at their work, stuff with short-term urgency that blocks them from doing fundamentally new things that require them to step back and make long-term investments, such as creating a plan for the year, creating a personal development plan, or rethinking and redesigning aspects of company strategy. Be aware, though, that the opposite can also be true: people can spend the majority of their time making plans without getting to the point of actually *doing* things. The worst-case scenario is when creating a plan takes so much time that reality overtakes the plan, resulting in people revising the plan over and over without ever implementing it. My experience however, is that the tendency to spend too much time on short-term urgency at the cost of long-term importance is the more common of the two problems.

> *The worst-case scenario is when creating a plan takes so much time that reality overtakes the plan, resulting in people revising the plan over and over without ever implementing it.*

When I first was confronted at work with the issue of staying focused on what truly matters while being bombarded with an endless number of small requests, it took me back to my personal experience of being a competitive fighter. I practiced many forms of martial arts from the age of five or six, among them judo. In judo, you have an opponent who is always trying to pull you in all kinds of directions, while you, of course, have your own clear objective of conquering that person. When you step into your first competitive judo fight against a strong opponent, it feels as if you are walking into a big, strong whirlwind. As soon as your opponent gets a grip on you, it is very easy for you to lose your focus and be dragged around, but you can't allow that, of course. You need to keep your head cool and control the match. That is not just a matter of dictating and forcing your opponent in a desired direction, though. You can control and steer an opponent only if you continuously keep feeling his balance and keep reacting to his quick actions, so you need to be open and flexible while clearly leading the match in the direction you desire.

It is the same in business. You shouldn't lose yourself in every random request that comes in, yet you can't shut all of it out either. I therefore built a model that helps you stay focused under any pressure by learning from the best: the ancient Japanese samurai warriors. In my previous book, *Samurai Business,* I described a powerful ABCD model for a sustainable strategy that originates from martial arts but has strong relevance for your work environment as well. This model describes the four forces of alignment that you need to control at all times in order to keep your head cool so that you can focus on things that matter to you and to the company, while staying in contact with your environment. The first and central factor of that model, awareness, was already covered in the previous chapter. Awareness helps you define who you are, what your objectives are, and how those relate to your business environment. With the right awareness as a starting point, the other three forces (*balance, center control*, and *distance control*) will make sure that the simultaneous alignment between your own goals and those of the people around you is

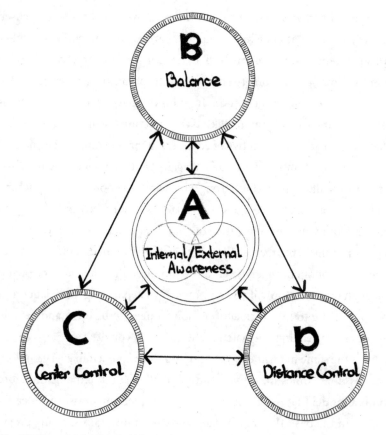

The ABCD model for sustainable strategy originates in martial arts and helps you connect to people from the heart of your strength, so that you keep focusing effectively on the right things despite any pressure.

"always on." That way your good intentions really happen, even if you step into an environment of complete chaos. Awareness has a similar central role in battle, which is why many practitioners of Japanese martial arts practice Zen meditation.

> *You shouldn't lose yourself in every random request that comes in, yet you can't shut all of it out either.*

BALANCE

The *B* in the model stands for *balance*. In martial arts, you can unbalance an opponent only if you are balanced yourself, and you can keep your head cool during the fight only if you are mentally balanced. Both physical and mental balance are important in business. To achieve them, it is important that you always know what you think you can or are willing to deliver compared to what will be expected from you. The answer to this question will be different, depending on your life and career phase. Your view on working long hours, for instance, may vary, depending on whether you have a life partner or not and whether you have kids or not. If you are single, your work may be an important ingredient of your social life; hence, you may be more open to working late often and joining social events related to work. You may be more willing to move abroad for a new job or have a longer commute. How much you can handle may also depend on your health. I remember that at the beginning of my career I did not care at all about how hard I needed to work or what projects I took on, as long as I felt they were adding to my experience. Later, however, I became more careful about how I spent my time. This was partly because I became more conscious of the value I was adding, but it was also because I had experienced moments when I had an increased heart rate and became ill as a result of working too hard for sustained periods. Once you realize that there are limits to what your body can do, it makes you think differently about your workload. Be aware that work pressure is not always a matter of working long hours; it can also involve something like work atmosphere or accountability. A job with heavy office politics or hard targets may make some people feel pressured, while others in the same situation feel a sense of excitement or a drive for achievement. It is up to you to monitor your balance at all times: Do you feel comfortable with the things that are being asked of you? You are the only one who can decide how much work pressure is acceptable to you. That knowledge alone should help you resist pressure at moments where that matters.

Luckily, as you build your individual skills, you have more to offer a company, so you are in a better position to resist the pressure that people put on you, and you can even make demands, too. This means that you can, for instance, specifically ask for projects that you enjoy working on and refuse to work on other types of projects. In exchange, you offer your dedication and your skills.

Be aware that there is a trade-off between balance and risk taking. If you always choose the safe route, never diving into something if you are not 100 percent sure you can deliver, your development is likely to be slower than the potential you have in you. At some point in your career, you may find that the range of choices open to you is limited to the exact things that you have already done and that you may not enjoy anymore at that moment in time. On the other hand, too much risk taking may take you into situations where you cannot deliver what is expected of you. This can make you unhappy or even harm your health and may result in your losing your job. At each moment, seek to find a balance between taking a leap into the unknown versus taking a step back and building on things that you already know and can do.

> *Be aware that there is a trade-off between balance and risk taking. If you always choose the safe route, never diving into something if you are not 100 percent sure you can deliver, your development is likely to be slower than the potential you have in you.*

CENTER CONTROL

The *C* in the model stands for *center control*. In martial arts, center control means that you connect to your opponent from the core of your strength. Imagine yourself opening a jar of jam with the lid stuck. You'll see that your hands will automatically move in the direction of your belly button—not sideways, not upward, but straight to the center. This is where you are strongest and where you can apply the most force. This is why any technique in martial arts is initiated from the center of your body, whether it is a blow, a kick, or a throw. The previous two factors (awareness and balance) give you the right basis for establishing center control in all aspects of your professional life. If you do these two things well, you'll have a clear image of what you want to achieve in both the short and the long term, which qualities will help you get there, and how much you are willing to sacrifice to do it. With that knowledge, you can face any moment of decision with confidence. This applies to both big decisions, like the decision to accept or reject a new job, and small decisions, like helping someone with a small request or not.

Every time someone approaches you with a request, you can take a small step back and reflect quickly: What is it that this person wants? And how does that relate to what *you* want? How does that help you decide what to do next? The confidence that comes from knowing what you want and what is important to you helps you to be more open and relaxed when you are listening to what others want from you, even if you know you have to say no. If the no is a conscious trade-off against other things that are important to you, it is easier for you to explain your priorities, and even a gentle no will sound powerful. If a conscious trade-off results in a yes, people will be more grateful for what you offer them. The center of your strength is the ability to make conscious trade-offs between your priorities. If you connect to people from that center, they will respect you more, whether you say yes or say no. As a result, you will feel stronger and more in control. This again makes you more flexible in finding creative solutions to conflicting objectives.

> *The center of your strength is the ability to make conscious trade-offs between your priorities. If you connect to people from that center, they will respect you more, whether you say yes or say no.*

DISTANCE CONTROL

The *D* in the model stands for *distance control*. In martial arts, you can completely dominate a fight by keeping your opponent at a distance that is optimal for you but not for him. A tall boxer will often keep his distance by using quick jabs, while a short boxer is more likely to close the distance quickly by diving under a sweeping arm to land some punches. In professional life, distance control is about explicitly managing expectations. This alignment skill again builds on all the previous ones. If you know the qualities you have to offer, know the direction in which you want to develop and what you want to achieve, and are capable of making conscious trade-offs, the last step is explicitly *stating* these trade-offs. If you are discussing a potential new job with an employer, explicitly state what you hope to find in the job, what you think you can and cannot offer, and what you think you need to learn. At the same time, explicitly ask the employer what she expects from you and how fast you would need to deliver that. If you see mismatches between what others expect of you and what you can and are willing to deliver, address those mismatches and negotiate until both players are happy. If you can't find sufficient common ground, accept that this is just not the opportunity for you (or at least not for now). If a colleague approaches you with a request, ask him to be explicit about what he wants from you and when. Then check your priorities and state what you can offer. Will you support the request at all? If yes, what will you deliver, and when can the other person expect it? If you are not used to this way of negotiating about the efforts you have to offer, you may feel that it is an inflexible and too formal way of working; maybe it makes you feel like you are not being helpful. In the example of deciding not to take a certain job, you may feel as if you are missing out on an opportunity. In all these cases, try to remind yourself that clarity is very valuable, both for you and for the person you are talking to. If you say yes without managing expectations in this way, you may end up having to do so many tasks that either the quality of those tasks will suffer or you end up structurally working more late hours than you are comfortable with. This may result in your being unhappy and leaving the company at some point. For your colleagues, that may mean that the work you deliver to them does not come as soon as it could or is not as strong as it could be, and it may mean that they will lose a valuable colleague at some point. If people are clear about what you can and are willing to deliver, they can confidently plan their own work based on that. You will be a reliable partner for them, and as such you will be appreciated.

> *If you see mismatches between what others expect of you and what you can and are willing to deliver, address those mismatches and negotiate until both players are happy.*

With the right practice, the ABCD model will help you focus on the things that matter to you, to your colleagues, and to the company under any kind of pressure. That focus will ensure that your efforts are both useful and sustainable. In the beginning, this may require conscious reflection. You may have to sit down and put things in writing. You may need to set aside some time to have conversations with important stakeholders. This may feel like extra time and effort, yet that alignment will help you later set your priorities with confidence, since you know that you have the right backup in place. As you progress in your career and internalize this way of working, it will become automatic. It may even become your general attitude toward life and work. Every time something comes up that requires you to make a choice and a trade-off, you'll quickly reflect back to what is important to you and to the person in front of you, and you may be able to make your choice and manage expectations in just a few seconds.

Ultimately, you get what you pay attention to. If you pay attention to everything, you get everything at once. If you pay attention to annoying things, you get annoyances. If you pay attention to things that go wrong, that is what you get. If you pay attention to the objectives that you think are important, you will develop a relevance filter that grows in strength over time. If you have built the kind of alignment described in the previous chapter, you have all the backup you need to decide which tasks you do and don't want to invest time in. You can challenge anyone who pushes you to do annoying and irrelevant short-term tasks by referring to your aligned long- and short-term objectives. Some people will immediately acknowledge that you have other, more important things to do; others may get upset and keep pushing. However, if your objectives are aligned with those of all the right decision makers, it doesn't matter how hard people push.

> *Ultimately, you get what you pay attention to. If you pay attention to everything, you get everything at once. If you pay attention to annoying things, you get annoyances. If you pay attention to things that go wrong, that is what you get. If you pay attention to the objectives that you think are important, you will develop a relevance filter that grows in strength over time.*

Learn to monitor all four alignment factors all the time and you will be surprised to see how many tasks you can handle at the same time while retaining a feeling of complete control. Keep in mind that none of the ingredients of the ABCD model is redundant; if one breaks, they all break, and all factors change over time, so all of them need continuous monitoring. From time to time, for instance, you'll need to readdress the topic of awareness because your skill set changes over time, as do the skills that you enjoy using and the skills that have commercial value. The emergence of the Internet, for instance, has made many traditional skills redundant, while other skills have come to be in high demand. Make sure the skill set you choose to utilize and develop moves along with the developments in the field of work that you choose.

> *Keep in mind that none of the ingredients of the ABCD model is redundant; if one breaks, they all break, and all factors change over time, so all of them need continuous monitoring.*

ACTIONS TO REMEMBER

- *Awareness (internal and external).* Use the three-circle exercise to plot your personal qualities. Identify which qualities can be found in each circle. Identify the kinds of jobs and companies that would allow you to utilize those qualities. Formulate short-term, medium-term, long-term, and lifetime objectives for your career. Start talking to relevant people.

- *Balance.* State what you are willing to sacrifice for a job and what you are not. Monitor from moment to moment how comfortable you feel delivering what is being asked from you. Strike the right balance between taking risks and building on what you already know and can do.

- *Center control.* Learn to listen openly to people's requests and demands while consciously prioritizing potentially conflicting objectives and/or requests.

- *Distance control.* Explicitly communicate what people can (or cannot) expect from you and when, but also what you would like in return from them and when.

HOW AND WHY YOU WILL NEVER
FAIL A JOB INTERVIEW

This chapter offers you two simple but valuable rules that will help you never fail job interviews. I remember one point in my career when I had to do a large number of job interviews over a sustained period of time in order to find a job. That happened when I wanted to move out of my first job and start working in media and advertising. In the end, it took me about nine months to find a job, and I wrote more than 90 applications. The challenge lay in the fact that I was trying to change from a nonprofit environment into advertising. I had no experience in advertising, and this was a time of crisis, with unemployment, particularly among young professionals, being a big issue (similar to the situation many countries are facing today).

At that time, I was always very nervous when I went into job interviews. I had high expectations for my career, and I wanted a good opportunity to start building the right kind of experience. At every job interview, I felt that my whole career was at stake. I always tried to anticipate the kinds of questions that would be asked, and I prepared answers to all of them. In the conversation, I was always afraid that the interviewer would come up with a question I had not prepared for and that I might give the wrong answer. Hence, before the interviews, I felt nervous, which probably did not help me come across as a confident professional applying for a job that he was prepared for. As I grew older and more experienced, that nervousness faded away and I started preparing for job interviews in different ways. My attitude toward job interviews nowadays is completely different from what it was then. That is because I discovered two simple but valuable rules. These rules will help you to never give a wrong answer on a job interview and to face interviews as relaxed as you possibly can be:

- Rule 1. You need only one job.
- Rule 2. You are *not* there to ask for a favor.

Let me walk you through my personal experience: how I got to these rules and what makes them so meaningful. In my first job, I was working for a government sports organization, helping gyms in the fields of martial arts and strength sports to organize themselves better. I found that job by doing the awareness exercise and listing my skills in the three Circles of Awareness. The exercise at that time resulted in a list of skills that combined my passion for sports with the things I had learned at university about corporate communication and with my experience as a judo teacher. Of course, that did not immediately point to any standard type of job, since this was a somewhat unusual combination. However, these were the skills that I had and wanted to use.

The next step was trying to match my combination of skills, knowledge, and passions to a concrete job. I started talking to friends about how I wanted to combine the elements of sports and communication in a job. I asked if they knew people who were doing such work. Someone referred me to the person who was managing communication for the Dutch national judo foundation. I talked to him and asked him what kind of things he worked on, what he had studied, and how he got his job. I asked him if he was aware of any jobs that would allow me to combine the skills I had listed. I was lucky; he knew of a new project being started in which all the foundations in martial arts and strength sports worked together. They planned to hire account managers to visit their association members, which were martial arts clubs and gyms, to improve professionalism in their organizations and help them be successful. That sounded like a unique opportunity for me:

I applied for the job and got it. This first round of job applications actually went rather smoothly for me, and I found something that really fit what I was looking for at that time. Finding my second job was not so easy, though.

I worked in my first job for about three years and liked it a lot, but at some point I started to miss the opportunity to take the next step, and I did not really see role models around whom I could admire and learn from. I figured that I would find more of those people in commercial companies, since that is where the money is and thus where the people who have great skills go. Of course that isn't entirely true, yet that was my reasoning at that time. I started thinking about what kind of work interested me most, and I felt a fascination with advertising, although I had no idea what working in advertising actually meant or what kinds of jobs and companies I could find there. The topic just appealed to me.

Again I started to talk to friends to see if any of them knew someone who worked in advertising. I got referred to all kinds of people. One person was working in sport sponsorships, another was a graphic designer, and another had previously worked at an advertising agency as creative director. Through these conversations, I learned about the kinds of companies I could potentially work for and what kinds of jobs those companies offered. One person said that the job of account executive would be the best place to start in an advertising agency. With my lack of experience, though, it was hard for me to visualize what the job really entailed. Still, I decided to take the guy's word for it and made becoming an account executive my objective.

I soon realized that making the switch would not be easy because of my lack of experience in advertising. I knew I would have to make a big effort. To make things worse, there was massive unemployment at that time, and I had heard that companies typically received hundreds of applications for open jobs. However, I had read in *What Color Is Your Parachute?* that it is often wiser to reach out to companies even if they have no open jobs. That way, you aren't competing with so many people at the same time, and if they see something in you, they may decide that they are looking for someone like you after all. Instead of writing a regular letter, I made a small booklet displaying my education, my work experience, my personal passions, and what I was looking for in a job. I hoped that this would stand out in a pile of hundreds of letters. I made a list of 70 advertising agencies that I could potentially work for. Only a few of them had open account executive jobs, and every job description asked for two or more years of prior experience in that job. I applied anyway, and I also sent my booklet to the other agencies that did not have open jobs. I called each agency about a week later to verify that my application had been received in good order. In the first six months, I got nothing but rejections saying that I did not have the right experience, and often I got no response at all.

Particularly in tough economic times, companies often get hundreds of applications for a single job. That may result in your receiving many rejections or no response at all, but that doesn't matter; you need only one job, and you *will* get it if you persist.

I decided to broaden my scope to other roles in communication, so that I could at least make the switch from a nonprofit to a for-profit environment. I applied for about 20 open jobs in a variety of companies, and I started to get interviews. One interview was for a job as media planner in a media agency. I had read the job description, but again I found it hard to figure out exactly what the work of such a person would look like. I figured that it would be a good point of entry, though, since it was a junior role and was somewhat in the direction of advertising. The guy told me that the company had received 300 applications for the job and had selected about 10 people to interview. I had multiple interviews, and I made it to the end. I was told that I would get the job and that the company would send me the contract in the next week. Then suddenly I stopped hearing from the company. After two weeks of hearing nothing, I contacted it and learned that there had been a hiring freeze. Corporate policies prohibited the company from hiring any more people at this time, and the job had been canceled. You can imagine my disappointment. I had been so close, yet my hands were empty again! At the same time, the fact that I had reached the stage of getting a job offer without any prior experience and with a total of 300 people applying gave me some confidence about my potential to succeed.

About two weeks later, I got a call from a pharmaceutical company that was looking for an account manager. The company had received about two hundred applications and selected about five people to interview. Again, I did not know exactly what I was applying for despite reading all the job information (at the time, I figured that my inexperience made it hard for me to understand the nature of the job; today I know that job descriptions are often generic and unclear). After multiple interviews, the guys explained to me that they had decided to hire a different person who had more experience in this exact job, but that they liked my personality and ambition a lot. They felt I would be a better fit in a marketing job than as an account manager, so they had decided to ask their international organization if they could create an additional job for me; I would hear from their superiors within the next two weeks. About two weeks later, they contacted me, saying that unfortunately they were not allowed to create the new job. Again I felt the disappointment of being so close, yet having nothing.

I was 9 months, 90 applications, and about 30 job interviews further, and I had no prospect of a job whatsoever. I doubted whether I would ever succeed in making this switch to communication in the for-profit sector. It started to look like an impossible move. Three days later, I was invited for an interview for the job of media analyst at a media company. Two weeks later, I was hired, and all my worries were over. It was not exactly a job as account executive at an advertising agency, but I had found my entrance into the field of commercial communication. It turned out that I was even more lucky: after three months in my new job, I got a phone call from one of the bigger advertising agencies. The company had apparently saved my résumé for a year until the moment when it had an opening for an account executive. That moment was now, and the company invited me to come over for a chat. I was offered the job, and I decided to make one more switch, since this was the exact job I had set out to find. It was a long journey, but I succeeded in the end.

It is this experience that made me realize the first rule: you need only *one* job! It takes only one person to say yes for you to have the opportunity to take a step forward in your career. It doesn't matter whether it takes two weeks, three months, or a year. You need only one single job, and if you keep trying with patience and diligence, you *will* find that one job at *some* point in time. Even better: after you have that first point of entry, every next step will be easier. For every future job, you will be in a position where you have more experience, both in knowing what you want and in recognizing what you have to offer to a company.

> *It takes only one person to say yes for you to have the opportunity to take a step forward in your career.*

The second rule emerged as I got more experienced in the field of advertising research: you are *not* there to ask for a favor. You are not there to beg for a job; you have something to offer in return. After about eight years of experience, I became aware that I had developed a skill set that was rather unusual, which meant that I had something to offer. I did not want to settle for just any job; I wanted a job that was a perfect match for my ambitions for the upcoming years, and I wanted to work with nice people in a nice atmosphere. I was more conscious of both the skills I had acquired and the skills I still needed to develop. Hence, I wanted to have a job that allowed me to build on the skills I already had *and* that allowed me to expand my experience. I became more critical when going into interviews: I wasn't just trying to sell myself; I wanted to find out whether the job and the company were a good match for me and whether I was a good match for the job. That mentality changed my perspective in every job interview, since suddenly I was equal to the person sitting at the other side of the table. It was not just me begging for an opportunity. We were two people who were trying to get to know each other well enough to make a meaningful assessment of the value of working together. It was not just the interviewer asking me questions; I also had questions that would help me get a clear picture of what the job looked like, what the company looked like, what career opportunities there would be, who my colleagues would be, and who my manager would be. I have now had the opportunity to sit on the other side of that table many times as well, with me being the person who was offering the job. I have seen how hard it is to find good people and how happy we were when we found someone who seemed to be both a strong professional and a nice person to work with. All these experiences helped me see that an atmosphere of equality in job interviews is very important. That makes the conversation more human and takes away potential nervousness, so that you can be your best self.

Of course, it is easier to feel this kind of equality if you are an experienced professional and you know you have at least some specific skills. It is good to realize, though, that talented and motivated people are wanted at all levels of an organization and can be hard to find. In addition, a good match is based not only on talent and experience but also on your personality being a match to the company culture and to the people you will work with directly. Try to look at the people you are talking to as your future colleagues, as people whom you will work with every single day. If you actually get the job, you will see them as often as you see your spouse or your best friends. So it makes sense to assess whether you would feel comfortable as a person working with these people on a daily basis.

Try to look at the people you are talking to as your future colleagues, as people whom you will work with every single day.

Even if you are inexperienced and looking for your first career opportunity, realize that you always have something to offer. Realize you are not looking for just any job, but for a job that is meaningful to *you* and that makes you feel that you *want* to work there. Make every job interview a two-way conversation. With that mindset, you can never fail a job interview or give a wrong answer. If you give answers that are meaningful to you but that the person you are talking to thinks are rubbish, that probably means that there is not a good match between you two. If that results in your not getting the job, consider that a functional type of self-selection. I've been rejected for jobs that, with the benefit of hindsight, I realize that I never would have fitted. I didn't know that at the time, though. The company made the right choice for me, for I would have taken any job at that time. If at some point you manage to bluff your way into a job that you don't have the right skills for, it is *not* a win, for it means that you now have a job that is not the optimal fit for you. Similarly, looking at it from the other side, there is not much point in companies luring someone into a job by making it look nicer or different from what it really is. Both of you will be stuck in a mismatch, with all the problems related to that. Both of you should be looking for a truly sustainable match. That is what makes you equals.

Again, you are *not* there to ask for a favor; you are there to assess how nice and how valuable it will be for you and your future colleagues to work together. That mindset will help you be a pleasant conversational partner for the people at the other side of the table. Make sure you know what you are looking for. If necessary, do the awareness exercise to clarify that. Realize that most careers are a journey, so it doesn't have to be perfect from the start. If you commit to giving your search the time and effort that it takes to find what you want, it is inevitable that you will succeed. You need only one job, and, after all, the people on the other side of the table are looking for a great colleague, too!

7

THE THOUSAND-HORSEPOWER GROWTH ENGINE

O nce you've found a nice job, it is time for you to ramp up and grow into your role. This chapter will help you ramp up your growth curve at maximum speed. The first months in a new job are likely to be hectic. You'll often be overloaded with all kinds of new information, and it may be hard to distinguish what is relevant from what is not. You will find yourself having to deal with basic stuff, like filling in some insurance or pension forms and learning how the joint calendar works and what kind of processes and programs the company uses. At the same time, you need to get to know the people in the company by having introductory conversations in which you can ask many questions: Who will be your immediate colleagues, and what are they working on? Who are the senior people in the office who are important to you, and what is on their minds? What do they expect from you? What would be the best way to get going? What information should you read? What projects should you start with? Step by step, you will create a personal network and hopefully get an increasingly clear picture of what you should be doing within the company. People will send you stuff to read to help you get up to speed on important topics, but very often you will also be expected to ramp up your work immediately. This first phase of a new job can often be like having two jobs at the same time.

Besides being hectic, this ramp-up period is also very important, since you have to earn your first credits and make sure you're working on the right things. The ABCD model for sustainable strategy will help you take the first steps in managing complexity and developing priorities here, yet particularly in this first phase, doing your work goes hand in hand with acquiring new skills. These two things can sometimes be in conflict. If you dive straight into your work, you may find that you lack the skills you need to complete your tasks successfully and efficiently. On the other hand, if you spend too much time building your skills without ramping up the actual work you are doing, your colleagues may start to feel that helping you build your skills does not pay off. Particularly in the early stages of a new job, you will always need others to help you get familiar with your tasks and the things you need to know, but at the same time, everyone in an office tends to be busy. People are understandably careful about how they spend their time, so ideally you need to show them that you can help them reduce their workload if they help you be successful. You need to combine learning and doing as much as possible.

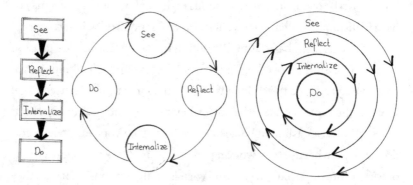

Acquire a model for learning that helps you continuously improve, even if your everyday workload is high.

The illustration visualizes three different ways in which you could organize your process for acquiring new skills and knowledge. If you recognize your way of working in one of the three flows, you are already in a good place. All these flows represent a process of conscious internalization of knowledge and skills rather than just copying what others do based on the assumption that their way is also the best way for you. If you recognize your own model in one of these flows, you may be surprised to hear how many people do *not* follow a process of this kind. If you ask professionals why they do things in a certain way, they cannot always explain it. If you keep pushing, you may find out that they just do things the way they were taught to do them without questioning why. Or they just found out that a certain way of handling things worked, without wondering whether another way would be more efficient. Hence some people keep doing their work inefficiently for many years without substantially improving it over time.

All the models in the illustration assume that you consciously look at the information that is given to you (*see*) and reflect on what elements of that are useful for your specific job, skills, and personality (*reflect*). Based on that reflection, you can then adapt ways of working to suit your own style and role; this may require some trial and error to optimize your personal way of working (*internalize*). After that process of internalization, you start building your own routines (*do*). Because of the conscious process you went through, you will always be able to explain to people what makes your routines relevant and how they would change if the task in front of you were to change. It is good to realize that different people have different styles of working, which means that any of these models could work perfectly for you, and there are also most likely a lot of different ways to describe your optimal learning process. However, these three models help to explain some common trade-offs related to how people acquire new skills and knowledge. If you are conscious of those trade-offs, you are in a better position to decide what works best for you from moment to moment.

The first of the three models displays the most basic learning process: one in which you are required to build a specific skill for your job, which you then perfect over time and continue to use. This model works, but it also has a risk: it is tempting to stick to what you know and can do once you've nailed it. Your existing skills then become your comfort zone, and consciously or unconsciously, you may limit your development by staying in that zone. The second model visualizes a continuous process of learning and developing. In this model, you start to acquire your next skill as soon as you have mastered the previous one. With a mindset like that, you will never get stuck in your career, and you will never be bored. There is one risk in that second model as well, though. The stages of the learning process are separate from each other, which is in line with my observation that many people need some distance from their existing work in order to find the space in their heads to acquire new skills. The problem is that many jobs do not allow you to take that step back to reflect and learn as a separate activity; hence many professionals revert to their existing skill set as soon as their workload becomes too high. I meet many people with lots of potential that doesn't come out because they are completely consumed by the daily grind. If the workload is always high, that often means that people don't develop as much as they would like and their work starts to drain them over time.

> *If the workload is always high, that often means that people don't develop as much as they would like and their work starts to drain them over time.*

This is where the third model comes in. In this model, seeing, reflecting, internalizing, and doing are parallel processes. If you can master this skill of parallel processing, your work will never slow down because you have to learn new things. The fact that you are learning while you are doing even makes your learning curve faster and takes your experience to a deeper level. You need one important ingredient, though: the courage to dive into new things without the safety of knowing beforehand exactly what you need to do. You'll need to trust that you can start a task without having 100 percent clarity regarding it. You'll need to trust that you will be able to find out what to do and that you can build the required skills as you go. You'll need to strike a balance between planning, learning, and doing by flexibly switching back and forth between those three processes. Particularly if you are working in a new and fast-changing environment, as professionals in the digital landscape are, this way of working is the only way of being successful.

But how do you know that you are not diving into something that you lack the talent or skills for if you don't have full clarity before you start a task? That is something you'll need to learn by experience, starting with small projects and taking on bigger ones over time. Through trial and error, you will learn to make rough assessments of risks and key milestones as well as the skills you'll need to achieve so that you can make an educated guess before you decide to take on a project. By making balanced assessments of risks versus needs, you are taking responsibility for a project, which generally means that you will be expected to deliver. So you'll need to trust yourself. If you can prove to yourself and the people around you that you can make balanced assessments and then commit to doing whatever is necessary to make a project succeed, you will increasingly get nicer projects to work on, and hence you will keep getting opportunities to broaden your skills and experience on the job. You basically will have created your own thousand-horsepower growth engine!

Working in a fast-paced environment that always demands that you learn new skills as you go and expects you to take on projects with unclear outcomes can be very stressful. You need a quiet mind and a strong focus if you are to succeed in such a situation: a mind that helps you observe yourself and your environment and reflect on both while you are in the middle of the action. I benefit from my experience as a fighter every day. A fight is a continuous whirlwind of complexity and unexpected events in which one mistake can result in instant loss of the match. My judo teacher introduced me to meditation at the age of 12, explaining that it was like having a small person sitting on your shoulder observing what you do while you are doing it. There was nothing fluffy in his explanation. He did not ask me to sit on a mountain and achieve some special stage of enlightenment. He called it "meditation in the marketplace": observing what you do, think, and feel and what happens in your environment while doing what you do every moment of every day.

I have practiced this skill ever since, and it helps me keep a quiet mind while being under pressure. For instance, I discovered that my mind became angry either at myself or at the environment if things went wrong. That anger reduced my ability to reflect and take appropriate action, so it slowed me down. I learned to observe difficult situations and difficult interactions with people without judging them, and this increased my speed of action enormously. You will always have good and bad moments, of course. If you feel that your mind is stressed, take some extra small moments during the day—for instance, when you go for a cup of coffee or tea—to look outside the window and focus on your breathing. Even if you do that for only a minute or even a few seconds two or three times a day, you'll find that it helps you face complexity and pressure with a calmer attitude. If you feel it is useful to you, start building some of these short moments of reflection and relaxation into your working days.

The last part of this chapter will help you add an unparalleled layer of depth to the things you learn and the skills you acquire. If you embed one of the three learning models (or a similar model that fits your personal style) into your ways of working, you basically have established habits that will help you transform information into knowledge, experience, and values on a continuous basis. Information becomes knowledge if you give it a meaningful place in relation to the framework of things you have learned before. It becomes experience if you experiment with the new knowledge and see what works for you. Finally, true depth emerges when your knowledge and experience are challenged by situations or people that do not allow you to get away with black-and-white answers, situations where things that you think you know seem to conflict. It is in those situations that you'll need to apply your knowledge and experience with strong skills of improvisation and personal judgment. You'll be forced to make trade-offs and decide what parts of your knowledge and experience are really most important. This is where your personal values start emerging. Your personal values are those principles, feelings, or ideas that keep giving you direction under any kind of pressure in any kind of complexity. They are your personal truth (until new experiences give you good reasons to adapt them).

If the things you do and say are rooted in your own knowledge, experience, and values rather than in mere information, there will be a depth and conviction to them that is unparalleled. So always be critical when information is given to you. Filter what is relevant to you and make it your own. That also applies to the information in this book. Nothing that I write is the absolute truth. It is my personal experience, shared as openly and honestly as I possibly can. Don't just believe my words (or those of anyone else). Instead, if you find that there is a ring of truth in what I am saying, experiment with it and reflect on it. Does it work for you at all? Or does it work better if you give it a slight personal tweak? Does it still work if you are challenged? True knowledge, experience, and values can be demonstrated only if we are challenged. In an environment of continuous change and competition, you will always be challenged from time to time. Make yourself ready for that. Don't settle for information. Transform it into knowledge, experience, and values of your own.

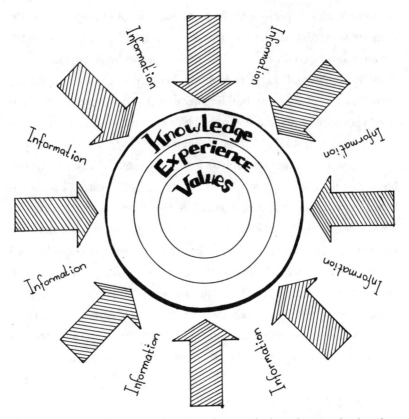

If knowledge is rooted in your personal experience and values, there is a depth and conviction to the things you say and do that cannot be acquired in any other way.

If you have the right learning habits in place, you'll feel that you are growing continuously as you take on new projects. Sometimes your existing role may not offer you the room to build the kind of new skills and experience you hope to build. In those cases, it can help to start side projects, either inside or outside your company. Inside your company, you could ask your manager if you can spend time working on an idea that you have. You may find people who see potential in your idea and are willing to help you with it. You may also find that you end up doing most of the work in your free time because your existing work requires your full attention. It will be up to you, then, to decide whether you feel that the investment is worth the effort and if you can handle the extra work resulting from it. Hobby projects that you do outside your company can add value to your work for the company. For example, I wrote a book about the integration of online and offline marketing that helped me gain credibility for the work I was already doing. While doing marketing for my book, I experimented with building my website, social strategy, PR, and search strategy, which put me in the place of a small business and made me ask myself the kind of questions that many of my clients face.

I personally feel that working on my hobby projects (like writing this book) is a form of relaxation. It adds purpose to the things I do, helps broaden my skills, and thereby enriches my future perspective. In a lot of cases, *not* doing these kinds of side projects produces more stress for me than having to spend the extra time on them next to my job. Hence I mostly don't feel bad if I work on those things during personal time. Of course, I also want to spend time with my wife, family, and friends and I like exercising, so I make an effort to balance those elements. These kinds of choices are all very personal, and you'll need to decide for yourself how you want to spend your time based on what things give you energy.

ACTIONS TO REMEMBER

- Assess what kind of model for learning and gaining experience you currently use.
- Evaluate the extent to which this model still works for you. Does it allow you to utilize your full potential? Are you happy with

your learning curve? Can you translate information into your personal knowledge, experience, and values?

- If you feel you want to work in a different way, assess what you would need to do to move into another model of learning and gaining experience. Do you need to step back more often to clear your mind for new things? Do you aspire to do a specific course? Do you fear stepping out of your comfort zone or starting projects with uncertain outcomes? Do you have the quiet mind needed to reflect on your skills while working under pressure? You might be much faster and stronger than you think!

- Design a trajectory of projects that can help you train yourself on the skills you want to develop, if needed by starting side projects.

PART III

CRAFT YOUR CAREER STEPS

THE JOB-CREATION FORMULA

When people are looking for a new challenge in their career, they mostly look for existing jobs and job descriptions. In many cases, though, the best thing you can do—but also the most challenging—is to create a new position that fits your particular goals and talents, thus enabling you to make the biggest difference for the company. Companies are always changing to adapt to their continuously changing environment, yet, as mentioned earlier, the environment tends to change at a higher speed than companies do. As the world changes faster and faster, new tasks emerge that are not covered in the existing company structures. If you can locate the gaps where a company is failing to carry out such tasks, you have found your potential next job. Sometimes you can even morph your existing job into your own tailored job, so that you don't even have to make a switch.

> As the world changes faster and faster, new tasks emerge that are not covered in the existing company structures. If you can locate the gaps where a company is failing to carry out such tasks, you have found your potential next job.

If I think back, many of my jobs emerged because organizations were changing (or failing to change) along with the landscape. I got the opportunity to work in advertising research because of the emergence of the Internet. Before that, research was mostly done with phone or paper questionnaires,

Companies are on a continuous journey into the future, like an unstoppable train. If you keep your eyes open for new developments, there will always be new opportunities to hop on that train in jobs that may never have existed before.

which were relatively slow and expensive to run. When the Internet emerged, agencies increasingly started running questionnaires online. This lowered the cost and increased the speed of data delivery and the amount of interaction you could have through questionnaires. After respondents filled in the questionnaire, the data would flow into an online dashboard where we could make reports for clients much faster than before. Our clients were typically top 50 advertisers that wanted to track how the performance of their brands was changing in response to their marketing and advertising efforts. Because of our online dashboard, we could measure advertising impact on a continuous basis, so we could help them make faster decisions that would optimize their strategy.

This type of active steering based on almost real-time research outcomes was kind of new, so no one was a real expert in it. This gave me the opportunity to step into a client-facing consultancy role working for the biggest advertisers, despite the fact that I still was young and had limited experience in research. Of course, I still had to prove the value of our research, but at least I got the opportunity to prove it. I would never have been given this kind of responsibility at such a young age in any kind of established business.

Another change in the business landscape helped me grow into a consultant integrating creative strategy, media strategy, and brand strategy. Creating a campaign concept and buying media space are two important tasks in advertising that were originally handled by one and the same agency. At some point, however, there was a split in the field of advertising. From that moment on, most of the time creative work and media buying were handled by separate companies: creative development was done by an advertising agency, and media buying was done by a media agency. I was lucky enough to have worked for both kinds of companies, and even though the tasks are different by nature, the creation of advertising and the process of media buying are still related and should be functioning in harmony. This often wasn't the case because they were done by different companies. For instance, if my research showed that a certain campaign was not effective, that could be dealt with either in the creative process, in the media buying process, or at the brand strategy level, depending on the situation. Very few companies evaluated these possibilities as one holistic picture, so I claimed that space. I started stressing the importance of integrated management of brand strategy, creative strategy, and media strategy, and I organized my presentations of research results around that triangle. This way of looking at these issues quickly resonated with clients, and I could build my professional profile around that.

Finally, my first job at Google also emerged because of a changing environment. Because of its increased use and bandwidth, the Internet became suitable for the kind of brand building that advertisers had previously done with TV, radio, magazines, newspapers, and outdoor advertising. In digitally developed countries nowadays, the Internet is the biggest medium in terms of time spent, and large advertisers are increasingly using websites like YouTube, Netflix, Vimeo, and Hulu in their brand-building strategies. The clients of the research agency I worked for therefore started asking me to help them optimize their budget allocation between traditional media and digital media. With my research colleagues, I designed an analysis that compared the effect and efficiency of digital versus traditional advertising. The clients loved it, and since a lot of those clients were also Google clients, Google started hiring us as its research agency. I worked on many Google projects, and then the company asked me to head up its research department in Belgium and the Netherlands. In that role, I dived into the topic of cross media and of changes in consumer behavior that were driven by the emergence of the Internet. I wrote a Dutch book called *Schizophrenic Marketing* about the gap I observed in many companies between digital marketing and traditional offline marketing. I described how companies were struggling to integrate the new and old worlds, whereas consumers blended them together naturally and expected companies to do so as well. This book received an award for best marketing literature of the year in 2013. The fact that the book received an award proves that companies are aware that they are lagging and that they aspire to change faster. That means that many jobs are opening up for those digital thinkers who have an eye for change and who make a proactive effort to step in at the right moment.

I hope my personal experience illustrates there are many ways in which you can shape your own job and career and use a changing environment to your benefit. Here are five steps that will help you create your own jobs as well:

1. *Observe and reflect.* People and companies have a tendency to get used to their routines. When people and companies have their first success, it is mostly because of a new insight that results in a new product or a new way of working. When that new way or product becomes a success, it tends to take on a life of its own. People will try to repeat the same things that led to the initial success; they may make some small alterations and improvements over time, but finding a fundamentally new idea suddenly becomes harder because it requires them to break away from their existing processes and ways of thinking. Reflect on a regular basis about the things that you, your colleagues, and the people in your field of expertise are trying to achieve: What

problems are people trying to solve, and are they still doing that in the most meaningful way? Give yourself regular moments to disconnect from your existing work and to talk to people with a mindset that's different from yours. This is where ideas and opportunities to do things differently emerge. Those ideas may be the starting point for your newly created job.

2. *Start making your unique contribution and communicate your success.* See how you can add value in the areas that other people consistently pass over, and start doing it. That may require you to make some extra effort and put in extra hours for a period of time. Fundamentally new ways of working are mostly not part of your job description, and you won't always have space to fit the extra work into your existing workweek. If you believe in your new ideas and are excited about them, spending extra hours to make them happen doesn't have to feel like overtime. If you can prove the value of your ideas by executing them and building some initial successes, that is the most powerful first step in the creation of your new job. You'll have to explicitly communicate how you've tried a new approach and how that has led to a success that otherwise would not have been achieved. If you don't do this, people may not notice what made the difference.

> *If you can prove the value of your ideas by executing them and building some initial successes, that is the most powerful first step in the creation of your new job.*

3. *Ask for more dedicated time for your new ideas.* This step can be hard and tricky, but it is crucial. Once you've proved that there is value in your new ideas and in your spending time on them, you'll need to get official permission to spend *more* time on them. If you don't do that, you'll always be working on your new ideas in your own personal time, and it is unlikely that eventually a job will be created that allows you to work on these (kinds of) ideas full-time. Without the right support and resources,

even good ideas cannot reach their full potential, so you'll need to reach out to the right senior employees, influencers, and decision makers to get their formal support and approval to transform your ideas into an official project.

4. *Eliminate existing work that keeps you from working on your new ideas.* If you successfully transform your ideas into an official project, you'll still somehow need to drop other things you are working on to ensure that you can spend the time needed to make the project a success. That can be done in one of two ways. The first option is to convince your superiors that your new project is more important than some other projects that don't add as much value and should therefore be stopped. If the existing projects you are working on are too important to be stopped, you'll need to go the second route, which is finding other people to take over the work you are doing or coming up with other ways to do it. In some cases, you may be able to simplify a process you were work-ing on so it takes less time or so less experienced people can do it. This approach has worked for me on various occasions. There have also been times when I knew we had a talented person on the team who would enjoy doing the work that I had been doing before. By moving on to a new project and allowing talented young people to take over my old projects, I could make room for them to grown in their careers. The growth opportunity we could give these talented young people was in many cases a strong argument to my superiors that helped me free up my time for new projects.

5. *Explicitly ask to create a new full-time job.* Once you have freed up time to work on your new ideas as an official project, you'll have the opportunity to create even more proof of success. Success tends to generate demand, which means that you'll need to spend even more time on your project. If you keep building, eventually you will get to a point where the project has been so successful and demands so much time and resources that it

justifies creating a new job (or in some cases even a new team) for it. Again, this is something that you'll need to ask for explicitly. Throughout the whole process of job creation, you need to be lobbying continuously, proving your success, asking for support, giving credit to those who have helped you, achieving even more success, and then finally asking for the resources you need. The ultimate resource is your new job. Once that job has been officially created, because you did all the lobbying and because you have already worked on the project and proved that you can make it succeed, you will be the most natural fit for it.

> *Throughout the whole process of job creation, you need to be lobbying continuously, proving your success, asking for support, giving credit to those who have helped you, achieving even more success, and then finally asking for the resources you need.*

There are probably many more things you can do to create your own job that I haven't mentioned. However, if you start with the five steps described here, I am sure you'll find your own way. You'll be able to consciously stretch your existing job to suit your skills and ambitions, and that is likely to result in new jobs over time. When you are systematically working on the five steps, you may discover that the company or manager you are working for is not willing to put resources behind your new ideas. If you truly believe that your ideas would add value and there is no room within your company to build on them, that may be your cue to start looking outside your company.

If you explain your ideas to other companies, you may find that they are more innovative than the company you are working for and are willing to create the required job that will allow you to work on your ideas. They may have already been thinking in similar directions, and you may just be the answer to questions that have been raised in conversations they have already had. If you consistently work with the right mindset, you'll encounter situations both inside and outside your existing company where you will be selected to perform a job that didn't exist before. A job that you have proactively created has benefits over existing jobs. For instance, because the job did not exist before, you can tailor it the way you want to, and since no one has worked on the topic before, there is always an opportunity to show that you make a difference. And finally, there are fewer people competing for a job that does not exist yet.

There are two don'ts when it comes to creating your own perfect job:

1. *Don't accept things as they are.* Look for what can be done better. Just because a corporation is organized in a particular way doesn't mean that this is the best way. Senior managers tend to always look for ideas to improve the company's ways of working. Do your own analysis, and see where the ball is being dropped consistently. Professionals are hired for critical thinking and proactivity. Use that to your advantage.

2. *Don't wait for jobs to be advertised.* If you wait for jobs to be advertised, you will find yourself in a long line of applicants. Start with the skills you have and like to use. See how you could use those skills to fill the gaps you are observing both inside the company you work for and in other companies. Then define what kind of job you can create to become the driver of change that CEOs are looking for. Also assess the kind of culture you want to work in, and actively approach companies with that type of culture or people whom you know within those companies. They may have been looking for someone like you and would be willing to create a position for you.

Finding the job that is a perfect match for you is similar to finding the right partner in life. Some relationships aren't easy, and things don't fall into place. Then when you meet the right person, you suddenly wonder how you ever settled for less. Over time, to keep the relationship fresh, both partners will be required to grow along with each other, just as your job should grow along with you. Nowadays most jobs are not for life;

however, even in a 40-hour workweek, you spend more time doing your job than you spend with your spouse, so it is always worth investing time and effort in doing something that you love and that fits perfectly with who you are and who you aspire to become.

> *Finding the job that is a perfect match for you is similar to finding the right partner in life. Some relationships aren't easy, and things don't fall into place. Then when you meet the right person, you suddenly wonder how you ever settled for less.*

9

THE BEAUTY AND RISKS
OF SWITCHING JOBS

The new generation of professionals is often accused of switching jobs too often, and some say that these people expect too much of their employers. In 2008, author Ron Alsop called generation Y "trophy kids," pointing to a trend in competitive sports and many other areas for frequent participation to be enough to earn someone a reward. Some employers feel that this is an issue in corporate environments and are concerned that millennials' expectations of the workplace are too high. I disagree that gen Y has expectations that are too high. In general, if you want to do meaningful work, you cannot settle for less. If you settle for a job that makes you unhappy, you won't invest in building great things for it, and it will eventually wear you out. So if you feel that your job does not allow you to do work that you consider meaningful, don't be afraid to switch jobs.

But is switching jobs too often a bad thing? Perhaps, if you quit a job because you've made a mess or if you leave on bad terms. But that being said, switching jobs can be an advantage when it is done carefully. It can dramatically increase the speed with which you move down the learning curve. Within a company, your opportunity to get a new position or a promotion is often based on time. It is not always acceptable to other employees if a young person overtakes others by getting too many (or any) promotions, even if that person is really that good. Switching to another company can be a solution to that problem, opening up the opportunity for growth again. If you are really as good as you think you are, your track record will resonate with other companies, and you may get the opportunity to step into more a senior position within a shorter time frame without your colleagues feeling that they are being overtaken. Beware, though: different companies have different problems, and in any new company, you'll need to earn your credits again. While your former colleagues knew about the great things you did for their company, your new colleagues may just see a new person coming in who needs to deliver some proof of his skill before he gets a seat at the table. Think where your prior achievements have the most value as you decide on your next step. In this chapter, I share my personal experience in switching jobs, and how the skills I learned in each job eventually built on each other to make a unique, clear, and very useful professional profile.

> *Switching jobs can be an advantage when it is done carefully. It can dramatically increase the speed with which you move down the learning curve.*

If you analyze how my various jobs created a career path, you may notice that I made many diagonal moves from one field of expertise to another that was closely related to it, mostly in a more senior position. Early in my career, that happened because I was in the process of finding out what kind of job fit me best, while later I had a clearer long-term plan behind my choices. My first job, as an account manager for sports organizations, helped me build my basic professional skills, such as organizing priorities, communicating with people, agreeing on actions with them, and building professional relationships, and I got a lot of practice in writing articles about projects I had worked on. After that, I worked first in a media agency and then in an advertising agency, which allowed me to experience both the creative side and the media buying side of advertising. It also showed me what it was like to work in for-profit companies. After that, my work as an advertising researcher helped me see the value I could create by combining all my previous experience and becoming an expert in research-based consulting about brand, creative, and media strategy. This was the first time I saw how much value there is in making diagonal moves. Rather than being trapped in one area of expertise, many more types of jobs had opened up to me, including the jobs I created myself. My switch to Google allowed me to get deeper insight into the digital aspects of marketing and advertising, and I could utilize the value of being someone who had worked in both the online and offline worlds. Finally, I noticed that researchers always have risk remaining researchers for the rest of their lives, so I chose the path of diving into (digital) marketing and branding and helping company strategies grow digital, which again opened new opportunities for development.

I always looked at my jobs as if I had a company within the company, shaping them based on what I felt I had to offer that was relevant to the people around me. Looking back, I could never have planned this exact career path in advance, yet all the pieces fit together perfectly, like a seamless puzzle. There are three important reasons for that:

1. I chose every single job based on a conscious evaluation of the skills I wanted to develop. The Circles of Awareness discussed in Chapter 4 can help you do so as well.

2. Regardless of how much I loved or hated the job I was doing, I always gave 100 percent and made the most of it until the very last day I worked there. There is no point in moaning about your job or leaning back if you don't like what you do. You are there anyway, so why not make the best of it? By doing so, you'll acquire all the skills the job has to offer you; you'll make a good impression on your employer, offering you the maximum opportunity to build a career *within* the company; and you'll also build a positive track record, offering you the maximum opportunity to build a career *outside* the company.

3. I never settled for too long in a job that did not allow me sufficient opportunity to develop.

Even if you can't envision a clear long-term career path for yourself yet, these three pillars will help you make job switches that will refresh and broaden to your career development without causing fragmentation on your résumé. With these pillars, every step of your career is a meaningful Lego block that allows you to build on all the previous ones. You'll discover over time exactly what structure you are building. You can look at your career and your skill set as a big Lego house. If you keep feeling a passion for the field of work you are in, you will always find ways to enhance that house: build some extra windows or add a garage next to it. If you feel that you have done all you can within a certain field of knowledge, you can always decide to build a new house next to it, or if you grew faster than you expected, you may end up building a whole city or country.

You can look at your career and your skill set as a big Lego house. If you keep feeling a passion for the field of work you are in, you will always find ways to enhance that house.

An important question to ask yourself is at what stage you should tell your manager that you are considering changing jobs. Should you tell your manager in advance at all? This can be a tricky question, but in general I'd say that there is value in keeping your manager up to date about all the factors related to your job happiness. This may include the fact that you are considering changing jobs.

> *An important question to ask yourself is at what stage you should tell your manager that you are considering changing jobs. Should you tell your manager in advance at all?*

Overall, even though companies should invest in creating a great work life for their employees, I believe that your job happiness is also your personal responsibility. You need to help your colleagues and superiors understand what you want. You need to flag problems or things that you don't like as early as possible. If you don't, you deprive the company of the opportunity to help you and keep you happy. If you flag issues early enough, you may be surprised how much your company is willing to do to make sure that you are in a role that is as valuable as possible to both you and it, especially if you have a history of doing great work. There also is a risk, though: there needs to be a certain level of trust between you and your manager if you are going to share the fact that you are considering a job change. If that is not the case, you may harm your opportunity for growth within the company, since your manager may feel that it is not worth investing in you when you are thinking of leaving the company. If you suspect that your manager may misuse the information you share, you may want to wait until you actually have the new job before sharing the news. That way, you still have the options of making the most of the job you already have or of finding a next step *within* the company.

Also, it is worth asking yourself whether your manager can and is willing to take any positive action with the information you give. The fact that your manager doesn't use the information you give her against you doesn't mean that she will use the information to create new opportunities for you. Not all managers are willing and able to help you find new opportunities within the company. If sharing the fact that you may leave is unlikely to result in new internal opportunities, that could be a reason not to take chances, since there is no potential upside. The only upside may be the fact that you keep your relationship with your manager good because you've made sure that she is not taken by surprise when you tell him you are leaving. Whether that upside is important enough to risk any potential downside is something that you'll need to assess yourself. You are in the best position to judge your relationship with your superiors. You may be able to discuss the topic with colleagues you trust, to get their perspective on the matter. You are the one, though, that still needs to make the final decision on what to share and what not to share. If you are in doubt, Chapter 13, which gives 10 office person-alities, may be helpful: if you recognize your manager in one of these char-acters, you may want to be careful with what you share.

When you are considering changing jobs, remember that no job is ever perfect. This introduces a weird contradiction: the best way to be success-ful is by doing something you like, so you should never settle for less, but every job inevitably has elements that you don't like, so a certain acceptance of that fact is required. The Circles of Awareness help you to be conscious of which parts of your job create the most value for you. If you know deep down inside that this is the right job for you, it will be easier to accept the annoying things that are related to it. The ABCD model for sustainable strat-egy helps you maximize the nice elements of your work while minimizing the annoying elements. Try to be aware of the things you miss while at the same time appreciating what you have. This will let you make the best deci-sions. Make sure you can always be confident that you gave everything you had in you to make things work, so that if you see more opportunity else-where, you have no doubts when you decide that leaving is the best choice.

> *When you are considering changing jobs, remember that no job is ever perfect. This introduces a weird contradiction: the best way to be successful is by doing something you like, so you should never settle for less, but every job inevitably has elements that you don't like, so a certain acceptance of that fact is required.*

I remember that at some moments in my career, I experienced feelings of guilt when I was trying to make the decision about whether I should stay or leave my company. It felt as if I was betraying the people who had given me a career opportunity. This was particularly true when I had been at a media agency for just three months and I received an offer of my dream job from an advertising agency. This decision was a hard one for me, yet I felt that I could not compromise my long-term career development for a short-term problem. I talked to my manager at the media agency and agreed that I would stay another three months, and luckily the folks at the advertising agency were OK with that. During that time, I did my work as well as I could until the last working day, therefore learning as much as possible about media planning. I later discovered how much value I had created by working for both a media agency and an advertising agency. Choosing my dream job at that time turned out to be the right decision, as did my choice to give my job at the media agency my best efforts until the last day.

It is good to realize that it is natural for young professionals to move on after a few years in their jobs. To a certain extent, companies are expecting that to happen. Particularly in junior jobs, the skill set you develop can be very narrow, so the time frame for growing in those jobs can sometimes be limited. If there are no opportunities for moving into other roles within the company, you would be limiting your learning curve if you didn't consider leaving. As you move into more senior roles, the nature of the tasks generally becomes broader and the time frame needed to establish meaningful results gets longer. My experience, therefore, has been that as I progressed in my career, I could spend more time working in the same job while continuing to move down my learning curve.

Now let's see what you can do if you bump into annoying things at work. If you are faced with things in your job that you don't like, you basically have three options:

1. *Change it.* This can mean convincing others to see or do things differently or finding a way to work around the problem so that it is no longer there.

2. *Accept it.* Accept that the problem cannot be solved and try not to be bothered by it.

3. *Leave.* Walk away from the situation, which could mean looking for another job inside or outside the company.

If you are confronted with something you don't like, you basically have three options: change it, accept it, or leave. If you fail to choose among those options, your feelings of happiness are likely to gradually degrade in one way or another.

Failing to choose among those three options basically leaves you with no choice other than to start moaning, which isn't beneficial to anyone. How long you should try to change or accept things that you don't like before you leave is completely personal and depends on the situation. It is your personal balance between the things you like and the things you don't like about the job or the company that defines what you should do.

To me, the cycle of making job changes tends to have three stages. In the first stage, I know for sure that I will not change jobs, no matter what opportunity arises. I have chosen my new job for good reasons, and I am dedicated to making it work. Even if a headhunter calls me with a job offer that would give me a 20 percent higher salary, I am unlikely to change jobs during that stage. I basically try to stay in this stage as long as possible by investing in shaping my own job and aligning with the people around me on how I'd like to develop within the company and how I think I can be most useful.

At some point, if there are structural things that I don't like and can't change, I'll start creating some parallel paths, such as having informal conversations with people that could result in a new job either inside or outside the company. Once that moment comes, a new opportunity mostly arises within the next six to nine months. During that period, I keep doing the best I can at my job, hoping that I can still change the things I don't like, and I make sure I remain valuable to the company. It is tempting to distance yourself from your existing job if your mind is partly somewhere else. Don't do that, though. Don't burn what you have, either while you are there or after you've left. There is a lot of value in finishing every job with a nice golden lining, even if there are things you don't like.

If I don't manage to find a new step within my company and the things I don't like continue to predominate, there is a third stage in which I wake up one day knowing that I want to quit my job as soon as possible. I basically don't want to be in that stage at all because I know it will make me very unhappy. I will feel trapped if I have to stay in such a situation for too long. The negativity coming from such a situation can block the positive energy you need if you are to find your next great step, and frustration can start to blur your ability to make balanced decisions. This is why I always save enough money to carry me through at least three months and preferably a year without working. For that reason, I also make sure that my lifestyle is not unnecessarily expensive. These steps give me the freedom to quit my job if I feel I need to, even if I cannot see the next step yet. That way I can keep my mind fresh and spend all my time on finding a next step that will give me positive energy again without being pressured to settle for something that just doesn't feel right. It is my safety belt that ensures I can always keep my momentum in making the right choices for my long-term career development, happiness, and health. The knowledge that I have this option keeps my head cool if the going gets tough. However, it is a safety belt I prefer not to use and luckily so far I have never had to.

The truth is that making career choices is always a bit of a gamble. There is a limit to how much information you can gather, and at some point you need to go with what your gut tells you. You don't have to know exactly what your next three jobs will be, but you should know roughly the direction in which you'd like to develop in the next few years or have some meaningful scenarios. This defines the type of building blocks your current or upcoming job should add to your overall path. So in each job, make sure that you do your best at it, no matter what, until your last working day. Then evaluate what you liked and what you didn't like, both in terms of job content and atmosphere and in terms of peripheral things like commuting time. For the parts that you liked, assess to what extent you had the skills to do those things and how you could create or find a job where you can use those skills more intensively. Clarify what each next job needs to add and what the role of the previous job was. Trust your own judgment. You are the one and only architect of your career.

You don't have to know exactly what your next three jobs will be, but you should know roughly the direction in which you'd like to develop in the next few years or have some meaningful scenarios.

10

SHOULD I STAY OR SHOULD I GO? FIVE SIGNALS THAT SHOULD ALERT YOU

No job is perfect, yet sometimes the issues that arise are so serious that you may decide that you need to leave the company. How do you know whether you should be a bit more patient or whether it is time to go? This chapter offers examples of situations that can be signals that should alert you and make you seriously consider leaving your current job.

Here are five signals that should make you think about whether you should stay or go:

1. There are no more opportunities for growth.
2. You can grow faster somewhere else.
3. There is a lack of trust between you and your manager.
4. You don't feel happy working with your colleagues.
5. The company's goals no longer align with your personal goals.

Let's dive a bit deeper into each of these.

Choosing to stay in a job or to leave it can be both exciting and scary.

THERE ARE NO MORE OPPORTUNITIES FOR GROWTH

The most important and most fundamental reason that you should switch jobs is a lack of opportunity for growth. To me, the opportunity to learn new skills and gain new experience is a key source of energy. Of course, this is not necessarily true for everyone. Some people are happy and relaxed if their work involves a familiar routine in a nice atmosphere.

I do believe, though, that personal growth is the fuel for almost everyone's *long-term* job happiness. Even people who enjoy a certain amount of routine will one day reach a point where they start feeling that they want to do something different. People are by nature not static; they change over time. If you systematically invest in personal growth, it helps keep you from someday getting stuck in a job that you don't like anymore. Personal growth opens up your opportunity to choose among jobs. I've already explained how you can stretch your existing job to open up opportunities for growth by helping your company adapt to its changing environment. Companies aren't static either, so your job should not be static.

> *If you systematically invest in personal growth, it helps keep you from someday getting stuck in a job that you don't like anymore. Personal growth opens up your opportunity to choose among jobs.*

There are limits to how far you can stretch any job, though. At some point, you may notice that your job requires you to keep doing what you did before and that the time you would like to spend on your aspirations seems to vaporize again and again. If you feel that your job limits the number of new things you can do, start thinking about your next step, either inside or outside the company. Keep in mind, though, that there are some points in your career when it may be preferable to stay in a familiar routine for a bit longer. You could, for instance, be going through some turbulence in another area of your life, such as having a child, moving, breaking up a relationship, or losing a loved one. House, spouse, health, and work are fundamental pillars of stability in people's lives. Changing too many of those pillars at the same time is generally not a good idea. Although you may not always have the luxury of choosing what you change and when, try to be aware of your personal situation before making a decision to change jobs. Every big change in your professional life can potentially cause a period of turbulence. However, if you can make a change that helps you retain or improve your personal and professional growth curves, you will be better off in the long run.

YOU CAN GROW FASTER SOMEWHERE ELSE

In some cases, you may still feel happy in your job, but you are not using your full potential. It is good to realize that sometimes you need to be in a job to discover that you actually can do it and to find out what you are capable of. When I moved into a client-facing role doing research-based consulting, I suddenly discovered that I was good at presenting to audiences and explaining things to people. Before that, I had always been shy when it came to presenting and speaking. I doubted the relevance of the things I had to say, and I didn't like being the center of attention. In this new job, though, I was paid to stand in front of an audience and explain what the research data meant for them. I had to present to audiences at least three times a week. Since clients were paying me to advise them, there was no need for me to actively grab their attention; it was naturally given to me. I found that I had a talent for reading data and translating them into understandable language. That gave me a story and allowed me to bridge the gap between the data and the audience. I remember the surprise I felt when I saw the positive reactions of the people who were listening to me. They accepted my thoughts and recommendations as if I had never done anything else. I became a trusted advisor for every client I worked with. When I was working in my previous jobs, I had never expected to be capable of doing that. The moral of the story is: you may be more skilled and talented than you think. People in senior roles have access to information that you don't have access to. They sit in conversations that you are not invited to. They use that information and those interactions as fuel for the work they do. It is entirely possible that with that fuel, you would run like a race car too. Try to visualize how your skills would flourish if you were in a more senior position, rather than judging them based on your current one. Then assess what potential you have and whether your current role still fits you. And sometimes you just need to take a small leap of faith to see what you are capable of.

Try to visualize how your skills would flourish if you were in a more senior position, rather than judging them based on your current one.

THERE IS A LACK OF TRUST BETWEEN YOU AND YOUR MANAGER

In many jobs, your manager is the most important person you work with. He can shape the content of your job and influence your rewards and growth opportunities. If you are lucky, your manager is also the person who can help you be successful in your role—for instance, by helping you build the right professional skills, by stimulating you to develop useful personal qualities, and by supporting you in establishing fruitful cooperation with colleagues. All these ingredients can make a huge difference in how you feel at work and how fast you develop.

The people I have seen building the fastest and smoothest growth curves were the ones who were lucky enough to have a manager who also turned out to be a personal coach. This is very rare, though, so don't expect that from every manager. It is important to acknowledge the value of having a good and open relationship with your manager, though. Try to invest in that while being both critical and thankful for what you get in return. Try to make it easy for your manager to understand who you are as a person, the context in which you perform best, and what career path would be most valuable to both you and the company. Then see what happens.

What you get in return may or may not be what you hoped for. If you get what you hoped for, consider yourself lucky. If not, in many cases there are understandable reasons for it. Managers always have to balance tasks: there are generally more team members that deserve attention, and in most cases there are multiple senior stakeholders whom they must please. Those senior stakeholders may in some cases limit the scope of your manager's influence. She might be willing to give you a certain career path but be unable to convince others to invest in that. If your manager can't offer what you hope for, it is not always a matter of unwillingness. Try to keep an open conversation together to evaluate mutual expectations regularly. If you structurally get the feeling that you are not being heard in those conversations or if promises are being made that aren't being kept, that may be a reason for you to start thinking about your next step. If your manager does not support you, despite your efforts at establishing the right relationship and despite your delivering consistent high-quality work, your opportunity for growth will always be limited.

> *If your manager can't offer what you hope for, it is not always a matter of unwillingness. Try to keep an open conversation together to evaluate mutual expectations regularly.*

YOU DON'T FEEL HAPPY WORKING WITH YOUR COLLEAGUES

You can make an assessment of the company culture when you're considering a new job, but you can't pick and choose colleagues the way you would choose friends. Your colleagues come as one big package, so it is pretty normal if you feel that some colleagues are nicer than others. Even so, in most cases, you spend a lot more time with your colleagues than you do with your friends, so you have to invest to make your relationship with them work as well as possible. In general you have three kinds of leverage that can make that work:

1. In the best-case scenario, you will be able to find some actual new friends. This may happen without conscious effort, but you can accelerate it by having random chats with people over coffee and lunch and by joining social events organized at work. At some point, you can invite your colleagues to your own social events if you feel that the right connection is there. If you feel that the time is right, consider inviting colleagues for a drink after work, a lunch outside the office, or maybe dinner at your

place. The atmosphere outside the office will help you connect on a different level and may allow you to discuss some things that are on your mind in confidence.

2. Some colleagues may not immediately appeal to you as potential friends but still turn out to be enjoyable to work with when you get to know them better. In many of those cases, you'll learn to appreciate them for who they are, even though they are very different from you. Sometimes that results in discovering a friend in unexpected ways, and sometimes it means that you will find a way to get along with each other as well as possible.

3. With some colleagues, you may never succeed in making the relationship work, and that may be fine for both of you. In the best-case scenario, you have the freedom to define how much (or how little) you want to cooperate with those people. You'll find that there is a spontaneous self-selection here. People who enjoy your company will make an effort to work with you more often, while people who don't will try to avoid you, and in many cases this is a good solution for everyone. Just make sure this kind of spontaneous avoidance does not harm the work you should be doing together.

In most cases, those three ways of relating will give you all the leverage you need to create a nice work environment around you. Such an environment can help to give you the pleasure, safety, and support you need if you are to keep delivering great work for your company. In the worst case, you will be forced to work closely with people you just don't get along with despite your best efforts. If that happens, it can become very challenging to keep performing well in your job, even if you like what you do very much. In the early days, when I was deciding on a job, my main concern was the content of that job, the things I was supposed to do, and the learning opportunities that would emerge from it. However, I have discovered that the people you work with are probably at least half the pleasure of your job. Having great colleagues can make almost any job nice, while having a fundamental mismatch with your colleagues can make you want to leave even the best job ever. For every job you select, try to personally meet the people you will be working with and assess how well they fit with your personality. In an existing job, make an effort to connect to people to build personal and professional relationships wherever possible. If you don't feel happy with your colleagues and you feel that there is little you can change there, start thinking about a change of environment.

> *Having great colleagues can make almost any job nice, while having a fundamental mismatch with your colleagues can make you want to leave even the best job ever.*

THE COMPANY'S GOALS NO LONGER ALIGN WITH YOUR PERSONAL GOALS

Company culture is an important ingredient in job happiness, but at the same time it is a bit hard to grasp. If you read job descriptions, almost all of them will say that the culture is open, fresh, and informal. If you ask people about company culture in job interviews, you will mostly get similar answers. You are unlikely to find many job descriptions saying that the office culture is hierarchical, political, and defensive. To get a good assessment of a company's culture, you will need to read between the lines. You can get a sense of the culture from many signals. What clothes are people in the company wearing? Are they walking around in suits, in casual clothing, or maybe in uniforms? That may say something about the level of formality within the company. Evaluate for yourself whether you would feel better in a somewhat formal environment or in a looser, more casual environment. Both can be either good or bad. Formal can mean professional, but it can also mean that the company is stuck in old-fashioned patterns. Casual can mean creative and forward-looking, but it can also signal a lack of drive and vision. There is no good or bad. You will need to read the signals in their context and then assess what fits you best.

You can learn more about company culture by asking people about their vision of the future, the direction in which they'd like to see the company develop. In a sales-driven organization, people might answer with growth numbers, while in an innovation-driven company, people might answer with their vision for future products or services. In socially driven companies, people may describe how they want their people to cooperate five years from now or how they want to change people's lives in positive ways. In the best-case scenario, you get a coherent view on how all three of these aspects of business will work together to develop a great company: a vision for making the organization commercially healthy by providing valuable products and services and by creating a great working environment for its people. You'll notice what the key ingredients of culture are by observing people when they speak and act. You can see people's eyes light up when they are talking about things they really care about, and their actions have more drive when they are doing things they care about. As long as you find something like an 80 percent match between your personality and the office culture, you will be in a good place. You always have at least some freedom to shape your own role. And realistically, some compromise here and there is generally inevitable. However, if the culture you work in feels like a fundamental mismatch with who you are, and if that makes you feel out of place on a structural basis, consider changing your environment. In some cases, simply switching teams within the company may fix the problem.

> *As long as you find something like an 80 percent match between your personality and the office culture, you will be in a good place. You always have at least some freedom to shape your own role.*

There are many other factors that can lead you to consider changing jobs, such as having too much work pressure on a regular basis or just the fact that you could earn substantially more somewhere else. I'll touch upon the topic of salary in the next chapter. Meanwhile, here are some questions that can help you assess whether you are still in the right job:

- Do you feel a certain eagerness to start working on most workdays?
- Can you provide value in your job in a way that gives you a feeling of purpose?

- Do you have the freedom to shape your job so that it grows along with you?
- Is your employer creating an environment that brings out the best in you?
- Do you enjoy working with your colleagues?
- Do you feel properly rewarded?
- Do you get the opportunity to develop yourself?
- Can you cope well with the workload you have?
- Can you step back when you need to?
- Does your employer empower you to make your own decisions when it comes to shaping your job?
- Do you feel that the senior leaders in your organization have a strong vision for the field of work you are in?
- Do the senior leaders in your organization have a view of organization culture that fits with who you are?
- Do the opportunities in your job match your short-term, medium-term, long-term, and lifetime objectives?

If the answer to all or most of these questions is yes, consider yourself lucky, for it seems that you are working for the right organization and are in the right job. If the answer to some of the questions is no, see what you can do to improve things. What are the things you like about what you do? What are the things you miss? Are there people in your environment who harm aspects of your job happiness? Can you approach them differently to change the situation? If the answer to too many of the questions is no and you do not see an option for improving the situation, you may want to consider seeking another job. You will probably be happier in a different position, which is better for you, for your employer, and for the people around you.

11

SALARY: HOW TO GET
WHAT YOU DESERVE

S alary means different things to different people. For some people, salary is the main reason for their going to work every day, while others feel that earning a lot of money is almost a crime. In particular, people who are working with passion tend to feel that salary is not their primary concern—and they are partly right, but they are also partly wrong. Your salary may not be what drives you, but the fact that you enjoy what you do does not have to conflict with getting paid well for doing it. If you are truly passionate about what you do, you probably put more effort than average into your job, and as a result you may perform better than average. If you acknowledge the value that you create, dare to ask for a suitable reward that is a symbol of the company's appreciation for your work and your passion. Appreciation is an important driver of job happiness, and if you are happy, your employer is happy too, since truly passionate workers are rare. At the same time, don't overplay your hand. A higher salary comes with higher expectations. If you are too greedy compared to what you have to offer the company, you can be sure that you will be under pressure soon, and your job happiness may suffer to such an extent that money will not be able to compensate for it.

> *Your salary may not be what drives you, but the fact that you enjoy what you do does not have to conflict with getting paid well for doing it.*

Salary means different things to different people, yet no matter who you are, if you do great work, you deserve great rewards.

Some people think that it is always the "shouters," the ones who continuously promote themselves, who get the rewards and the money. Is this really true? It sometimes is, but probably not as often as you think. The truth is that people need to enjoy working with you, and a manager can give you a promotion only if he knows that other people will feel you have earned it. That is the only way to give one person a promotion without making everyone else feel overlooked. If someone promotes herself heavily but fails to create really successful work and good working relationships, a good manager will notice the difference. Giving this person a promotion may do more harm to the team than good to that individual person. However, if you make sure that your work is relevant to the team and offer others the opportunity to also shine, more people will be happy for you if you get rewarded. Hence it will be easier for your manager to give you what you deserve.

> *A manager can give you a promotion only if he knows that other people will feel you have earned it. That is the only way to give one person a promotion without making everyone else feel overlooked.*

There is another reason why it is not always the shouters who get the rewards, at least not in the longer term. Any time you spend on self-promotion is time that you *cannot* be spending doing great work and developing yourself. In the end, great work and personal development are the most sustainable drivers of success and therefore of earning a good salary. Of course, it is not just you that needs to believe that your work is great; it needs to be relevant in the eyes of your colleagues and your superiors.

One of the things that can distract you from working on the right things is seeing people get rewards and promotions when there are good reasons to doubt that they really deserve them. Try to spend as little time as possible on this kind of thinking. It does not help you in any way. No one will give you a raise because someone else got one too, and you don't want to be in the position of talking down the work of your colleagues. You'll need to trust your own strengths and priorities. This is why the Circles of Awareness are so important. If you know deep inside that you are working on things that are meaningful both to you and to the company and that are a good match to your skills, you know you will be successful in the end. Then once your work is ready, because you care so much about it, you will intrinsically feel that you want to talk about it and show it to people, which is a nice and natural way of promoting your work.

Particularly in big companies or big teams, and even more in situations where your manager does not work in the same country as you do, some level of self-promotion is a necessity. It is impossible for senior leaders to keep track of all the great things that you and the other members of your team are doing, so you need to make it easy for them to see your contributions. Take some time every now and then to take your superiors and your teammates through your plans and to report to them when you achieve key milestones. When you are finished, summarize what you have worked on, what progress you have made, and what challenges you overcame. Then try to make the things you learned useful to others. That way, you promote yourself in a way that is useful both for you and for others. If you put effort into building great work, you are allowed (to some extent) to take pride in it.

> It is impossible for senior leaders to keep track of all the great things that you and the other members of your team are doing, so you need to make it easy for them to see your contributions.

Balance, center control, and distance control as described in the ABCD model are also important in getting the salary you deserve. These are the tools that help you to be conscious of the trade-offs in your priorities and manage expectations so that people can count on what you deliver. These tools allow you to be helpful when it really matters, and they support you in saying no gently yet firmly if you have more important things to do. Rather than reducing the credit you receive, each no will be a signal that you are working on meaningful things. You may still sometimes bump into unpleasant resistance because some people just won't take no for an answer, but even if that happens, the fact that you draw a line in the sand every now and then is important. Without it, your golden efforts and intentions would be like water; people would find it normal for you to help them with all kinds of small things, and you would fail to make a difference in things that are really noticeable. Without the sustainable strategy of the ABCD model, you can work an endless number of hours doing small, useful things without ever getting rewarded for it.

In the ideal situation, doing great, meaningful work and sharing it in the right way will automatically result in an increased salary and promotions over time. If you can build success and a good salary this way, you are in a great position. Your passion will ensure that you don't have to worry about salary, and your salary will ensure that you can keep focusing on your passion. Every now and then, you may need to explicitly ask for an increase in what you are paid. If you did great, meaningful work and made an effort to share that work with both your colleagues and your superiors, you should be in a good position to get at least part of what you ask for. The widespread knowledge of your work will make it easier for your manager to make a case to senior leaders for giving you an increase in salary and maybe a promotion. The fact that you made your work useful for your colleagues will help your manager justify a potential promotion to the other team members.

In the worst case, if you are convinced that you are not getting what you deserve despite your asking, you may need to force the company to pay you more by stating that you may leave the company if you don't get it. In fact, if you reach that stage, you might want to consider leaving without making that threat. Even if you get what you ask for, you are unlikely to feel fulfilled. It is much nicer to get a 5 or 10 percent raise without asking for it than to get a 20 percent raise by forcing people to give it to you. I have been in situations where a company offered me a big raise after I found a new job, but it never made me reconsider leaving. If delivering great work does not result in a raise but threatening to leave does, something is fundamentally wrong. It basically means that you'll need to negotiate and potentially threaten to go away every time you want an increase in salary, while it is much nicer to spend as much time as possible focusing on doing great work.

> *It is much nicer to get a 5 or 10 percent raise without asking for it than to get a 20 percent raise by forcing people to give it to you.*

Your happiness in your job and your potential for development are the things that really matter. Your salary is just one aspect of that. I recommend that you never sacrifice your happiness for a higher salary and also never sacrifice your personal and professional growth for a higher salary. If you do, you risk trading long-term happiness and success for short-term financial gains. That being said, there is nothing wrong with aspiring to a great reward for great work, so try not to deny yourself that.

> *I recommend that you never sacrifice your happiness for a higher salary and also never sacrifice your personal and professional growth for a higher salary.*

PART IV

DEVELOP INTO A MATURE AND APPRECIATED INDIVIDUAL

12

MAKING YOUR
OPINIONS VALUABLE

No matter how sincere your good intentions, your critical opinions may not always be received well. If you are a passionate worker, you may also be a perfectionist to some extent, a person who is seeking improvement all the time. You'll therefore find flaws more easily, and people may feel that you are judging them and thinking that they are doing things wrong. This brings the risk of your being labeled "too critical." Once you get that label, it can become increasingly hard for you to raise the bar of achievement for the company and the people around you. So picking your battles carefully and keeping your allies is extremely important.

This chapter gives guidelines for balancing a critical attitude with compassion and pragmatic thinking to guard your position as an appreciated professional, while retaining the strength to change the things that truly matter. These lessons include:

- Have respect for others.
- Pick your battles.
- Trust your judgment.
- Choose who will be open to hearing your opinion.
- Ask rather than state.

- Time your critical feedback.
- Balance critiques with solutions.

I'll dive a bit deeper into each of these.

HAVE RESPECT FOR OTHERS

This piece of advice may sound cheesy and paternalistic, yet it is the most important one I can give you. You can build relationships with other people only if you truly respect who they are and what drives them. You can respect people even if you don't like them. Respecting people does not necessarily mean that you look up to them. It basically means that you accept them as they are, even if that is different from what you like. However, respecting people doesn't diminish your ability to confront them about things you think they should do differently. On the contrary, respect strengthens your ability to convey your opinions. If you try to convince people of your opinion while judging them based on who they are or what they do, they are unlikely to listen to you. Hence, they will not make a change unless you force them to do so, and when you force people to do something, you always lose credits.

People feel it when you are judgmental about them (or about others), and most people react to that by either pushing back, shutting you out, or just disconnecting from you. They are more likely to be open to critical feedback or great ideas if they know that you have at least tried to see the world through their eyes. Not everyone is the greatest communicator, so sometimes seeing someone else's view requires you to put in some extra effort to really get to the bottom of what the person is trying to say. Try to see the good things in people, see their good intentions, and find at least one thing you can learn from every person you work with. Everyone has his own unique skills. Seeing them helps you understand where people are coming from. Someone who is coming from a different angle can shed a surprising light on matters. Seeing all perspectives will make you more well rounded and mature as a professional and will allow you to build valuable work relations.

> *Try to see the good things in people, see their good intentions, and find at least one thing you can learn from every person you work with.*

PICK YOUR BATTLES

In my work, I tend to always have a clear picture in my mind of how things should be, how challenges should be overcome, or how ideas should be realized. That makes it very tempting to try to convince people of every single aspect of that vision. I have discovered, though, that if I am too focused, always trying to get everyone to follow the path that I think is perfect, it can reduce my ability to get cooperation and realize my vision. Business topics generally have many stakeholders, some of whom may need to make trade-offs that are different from yours. Thus, things won't always be as perfect as you may think they could be.

It helps if you learn to look at business situations as a matter of negotiation rather than an all-or-nothing game. Not all aspects of your vision are equally important. Similarly, if other people have a vision of their own, not all aspects of *their* vision are equally important. Prioritize the things you want to change. Use less important things as material for negotiations; you'll have some things that you can give away in exchange for people accepting your view on the matters that are most important to you. If it isn't necessary, don't force people to give up things that they don't want to give up. This way you can focus your persuasive powers on exactly those topics that really matter to you while allowing others to do so as well. That way everyone comes out of meetings a winner.

> *It helps if you learn to look at business situations as a matter of negotiation rather than an all-or-nothing game.*

Of course, you will face situations where you'll need to convince people to give up things that *are* important to them. In those cases, it also helps if you have things to trade, so that they feel that you are giving up things too. Explicitly express your understanding and thankfulness for what they are giving up. Compensate them for that wherever you can, perhaps by making them part of your success and giving them credit for it or by helping them out with things that are meaningful to them.

TRUST YOUR JUDGMENT

Self-doubt can either make you stay quiet when you need to speak up or lead you to overdo things when you would have been stronger with a more gentle touch. In the early days of my career, I was always afraid that people wouldn't buy into my ideas. I therefore practiced in my head, building the strongest possible arguments that I could think of. Without that, I didn't feel safe expressing what I had to say. As a result, it took some time for me to open my mouth in conversations, and when I finally did, a big persuasive story would come out all at once like a slap in the face, leaving people very little room to think otherwise. I basically confronted people with my thinking rather than guiding them through it. As I became more confident as a professional, I learned to be more subtle. I spoke earlier in conversations, dropping particular aspects of my view step by step when they were relevant to that specific stage of the conversation. This meant that I was more open to adapting my ideas as the conversation moved on and I could present aspects of them that were relevant to what other people were proposing.

> *Self-doubt can either make you stay quiet when you need to speak up or lead you to overdo things when you would have been stronger with a more gentle touch.*

If you are confident of the value of what you have to say, you will connect to people from the core of your strength. That means that you'll be able to apply more persuasive power with less force. You will help them understand you rather than push them to do so. If you feel that you lack the confidence to express your opinion, you have already made a great first step. Seeing the problem is a big part of solving it. Try to approach the issue like a game. The topic becomes less heavy if you take yourself a bit less seriously. You can take small steps to practice your skills at expressing your view. Start explaining what you think in informal one-to-one conversations, perhaps over lunch or when you are with friends. Gradually extend that to more formal conversations and group meetings. Don't rush or judge yourself; give it the time that it needs. If you keep practicing and remain patient, there is no thinkable outcome other than success.

> *If you feel that you lack the confidence to express your opinion, you have already made a great first step. Seeing the problem is a big part of solving it.*

Trust in the value of what you have to say: train yourself to speak up in meetings with the right balance between assertiveness and calm confidence.

CHOOSE WHO WILL BE OPEN TO HEARING YOUR OPINION

If you believe in the value of your opinion, you will stop selling it and start considering it to be a gift. Such a gift is something that you want to give only to people who can appreciate its value. If you start with the people who are open to your story, you will get great practice in how to convey it. These people might ask valid questions that will help you increase the relevance of what you have to say. They may raise objections that could have taken your whole idea off the table if you had presented it in a formal meeting with people who have stakes that conflict with yours. In this stage, though, you can still try it out informally and work with others to see how you can overcome the objections that are raised.

The fact that your first trial audience is open to what you are saying will help you build the confidence you need if you are to convince people who are less open to your opinion. You might even discover that some people in your initial test audience see so much value in your opinion that they are willing to join you in convincing others that need convincing. Everyone has her unique skills; you might be the one with the good idea, and others may be the ones who know how to guide that idea through the organization.

> If you believe in the value of your opinion, you will stop selling it and start considering it to be a gift.

ASK RATHER THAN STATE

If you find that your opinion deviates from those of others, try to find out how they came to their conclusion rather than starting right in and seeking to convince them to think differently. When you do that, you prove to them that you are making an effort to look at the issue through their eyes, and you earn their respect by showing them that you respect *them*. At the same time, you discover whether there is information that you may have overlooked or whether other people just need to make other trade-offs based on different priorities. This knowledge helps you position your ideas in the right way to ensure that they have maximum relevance and create minimum resistance among all the people present. In many cases, if you ask enough questions, the differences of opinion turn out to be much smaller than you initially think. There may even just be a misunderstanding. For instance, people can sometimes be very sensitive to the specific wording you choose, giving it a different meaning from what you intended. Just by clarifying what all parties mean if they use certain wording, you may uncover misunderstandings; once they are eliminated, you can focus on any remaining real differences of opinion. Once everyone is on the same page regarding what the conversation is about, it is often much easier to find common ground.

TIME YOUR CRITICAL FEEDBACK

Stating your opinion at the right moment and to the right people is a crucial ingredient in successfully conveying it. If you confront someone with a mistake in front of a big group, for instance, you may make that person lose face when you had no need to do so. That, of course, makes it a lot less likely that he will accept what you are saying. You could have been more effective sharing what you think in a one-on-one conversation after the group leaves. Make people lose face in front of others only if there is really no other way.

In other situations, you may have something to say that is so different from where people's thinking is at that moment in time that they need some time to digest it. If that is the case, there is no point in pushing. Give it some time. They'll reopen the conversation later, or you can do so yourself. In general, there is a lot of value in practicing saying only things that are relevant to the people who are sitting in the room at that specific moment in time. Make sure you are aware of the agenda of the meetings you sit in and of the personal agenda of each individual in the room.

Don't fall into the trap of saying something just because you feel you have to say something. Make sure that your input matches the topic of the meeting and that you are in a group of people to whom it is relevant. If you are not, try to get the relevant people together at a different time.

> *Don't fall into the trap of saying something just because you feel you have to say something.*

If you fail to be sensitive in assessing which information is relevant when and to whom, you risk building a reputation as someone who is always coming up with useless objections and problems or who just talks too much rubbish. If this happens, people will increasingly interrupt you in the middle of sentences or will be more reluctant to let you speak in meetings at all. Learn to time and target your messages better and you'll see your reputation become that of someone who always has something useful to say. You'll find that you are having less difficulty getting people's attention. Just the fact that you inhale and move your body a bit forward before you say something may be enough for people to give you the opening to speak.

BALANCE CRITIQUES WITH SOLUTIONS

In general, there is not much use shouting that things are wrong without offering possible solutions. It is not your opinion (or anyone else's) that matters; what matters is the great work that you are trying to create together, so keep focusing on making that happen. If you object too often without offering solutions or compliments, it makes you look negative and takes the energy out of conversations. You may find that people will become less open to cooperating with you. Do not fight just for the purpose of being right. Focus on the common objective and all your interactions will be much more enjoyable and fruitful. Do that and you'll contribute to the creation of an environment in which everyone feels welcome and encouraged to share their knowledge and efforts for the common cause. In some cases, you may feel that something is wrong without knowing exactly how to fix it. In those cases, it can be OK to say what you think is wrong without offering a solution right away. Explain what you think, and say that you would like to think of a solution together. Ask if others agree that there is a problem and what their analyses of it are. If enough people feel that you've touched on a relevant topic, you may be able to find a solution right then and there, or if the topic is more complex, you may decide to make it an action item for a later meeting.

> *Focus on the common objective and all your interactions will be much more enjoyable and fruitful.*

If you manage to acquire the skills described in this chapter, you'll gather an army of people around you who enjoy working with you and who see value in you, both as a person and as a professional. Those people will be a valuable source of energy to get up for every morning. You will feel encouraged to use and improve your skills to achieve for common goals. If you have a bad day, they will be there to support you. If you need to take risks, they will have your back. And if you build success, you can celebrate together!

13

TEN PERSONALITIES: HOW TO RELATE TO YOUR COLLEAGUES

Even if you work on the right objectives in alignment with company goals and with positive energy, some people will be harder to get on board than others, and some people may be nicer to cooperate with than others. If you feel that cooperation with someone isn't as smooth as you'd like it to be, try to put yourself in the position of that other person and see if you can make it work better. Each person may have his own reasons for being less cooperative and may not even be conscious of how you feel. Some of your colleagues may consciously or unconsciously be worrying about what will happen if your ideas change things that have been working fine for them. For some people, behaviors that you experience as annoying are actually a logical choice given the trade-offs that they need to make in their job. Everyone has his own objectives and his own way of getting there. Some people are under much more pressure than you think, and that pressure can affect how they relate to others.

This chapter offers profiles of 10 personalities that, depending on what kind of a person you are, may sometimes be hard to work with. These profiles will help you to quickly assess who the people around you are and why some of them might not be as easy to work with as you'd hope. It offers ways to connect with your colleagues and better understand them so that you can work in a better atmosphere and be more productive together.

Please keep in mind that these examples are to some extent caricatures. I inflated certain recognizable aspects of people's characters to make them easier to spot. No one is a caricature, though. Always make the effort to look at people as they really are without putting them in some kind of box. Rather than getting annoyed by things you don't like about people, it is better to just observe them and overcome issues by reaching out to the full person, not just focusing on the specific behavior that annoys you. In many cases, things that annoy you about people are related to useful skills that they have and that they use to survive. For instance, someone who is very good at organizing things may annoy you by being inflexible if things need to be improvised, and someone who has the power to make big projects happen can make you feel like you are being pushed too much. If you can see how people's "annoying traits" are inevitably connected to their strengths, it becomes much easier to accept them and make the positive side of the skill work for you both, even in situations where you do not click naturally with a person. Luckily, you are very unlikely to meet people who are as extreme as those described here. It is more likely that you will encounter some milder versions of these personalities every now and then, so reaching out shouldn't be too hard. In the personality descriptions, I will offer some tips on how you can improve cooperation with each specific type. These are things that, in my experience, can help or that I have seen others do successfully to bring people closer together. Check whether what I say resonates with your personal experience, or at least has a ring of truth in it for you. Then experiment to find the best ways to connect with the people who work for you personally.

> *If you can see how people's "annoying traits" are inevitably connected to their strengths, it becomes much easier to accept them and make the positive side of the skill work for you both.*

1. Opportunistic Olivia

Opportunistic Olivia prefers to cut corners at the cost of fundamental long-term improvements.

Opportunistic Olivia is more likely to be nice to you if she needs something from you. She takes good care of herself, but she sometimes leans too much on other people. She may want to cut corners if that can get her short-term rewards or recognition. In some cases, however, her inclination to cut corners may be damaging to projects that aim to do fundamentally new things. Projects of this kind generally don't offer short-term benefits and also don't allow shortcuts.

If you are a pleasant and useful colleague, Olivia will generally be a great colleague to you because she knows that she might need you at some point in the future. Olivia is well connected, social, and smart, and she knows how to get things done. She is generally well organized and can be a good negotiator. She is not afraid of taking risks and may even enjoy taking them. If you have common objectives, she can be a great asset in getting all the important people involved in your projects. If you have a great idea, she'll recognize it, yet if that idea requires investment, you'll need to convince her of the potential glory at the end of the project. When you are working together, make sure that you keep an eye on the things that really matter for the long term. If Olivia asks you for a small favor, be aware that this favor might be bigger than it initially was presented to you and that you may not always get a favor in return.

2. Collateral Damage Danny

Collateral Damage Danny thinks that casualties are part of the game when it comes to achieving business goals.

Collateral Damage Danny is someone who's willing to get close to or even cross ethical lines to achieve business goals. He can be charming when he has to, but he generally has little interest in people. If your project is opposed to Danny's business objectives, he is unlikely to back off when trying to stop you from succeeding. The good thing is that his attacks are never personal, and he will always be open to reasoning. Business and personal matters are two completely separate things in Danny's eyes. If you focus on the common objective rather than on being right or pursuing your personal goals, you usually should not have a problem. If you and he are working on common objectives, you can expect very useful support and advice.

Danny has an extremely sharp nose for commercial opportunities, he is a strong negotiator, and he is competitive and goal oriented. If you have a unique skill set, he is likely to notice that and find ways to make it valuable, which can create great opportunities for you. Stay rational and focused when working with Danny; emotional arguments don't really resonate with him. If Danny needs something from you, he is likely to ask for it straight out. He may put pressure on you to deliver if he thinks you have other priorities. If you really have other priorities that are more important, don't say yes just because of the pressure he puts on you. Danny is a reasonable guy and will understand it if you have solid reasons to say no and you can explain them clearly. He'll most likely respect you for justifiably resisting his pressure.

3. Judgmental Jenny

Judgmental Jenny loves to gossip, particularly about new or lower-ranked colleagues.

People like Judgmental Jenny tend to organize themselves in small cliques that have little social interaction outside of their group. They gossip a lot. They are friendly upward in the organization, but not downward. If you are new to the company and you try to change things too fast without their being accepted by Jenny and her friends, you may find yourself isolated very quickly. Jenny has a clear opinion of how people should act and think, and what their morals and standards should be. If you deviate from the average too much, she may see you as weak, arrogant, weird, lazy, stupid, and possibly many other things. If you can ignore this and connect with her, treat her with respect, and show her who you really are, you may have a great colleague forever, though.

Jenny can be very dedicated to her job; she is good at what she does, but she may have a tendency to work in her comfort zone too long. She is judgmental not only toward others but also toward herself, and therefore she tends to be a perfectionist. Because of this, she becomes nervous if she has to work under pressure. If you propose fundamental new ideas to her, she may not be one of the first to join. She tends to see the risks associated with new ideas before she sees the potential benefits; however, since she is good at what she does, her assessment is definitely one to listen to. The objections she raises are likely to be real ones that need to be overcome. Just be careful; she may see obstacles as being bigger than they really are, so try not to be discouraged by that. Take her advice to optimize your ideas and show her that you are dedicated to finishing your projects until the very end and you will win her trust and support.

4. Laid-Back Luke

Laid-Back Luke has an easygoing personality. He is the last to come in and the first to go out—unless drinks are involved. Anything that might create extra work, like a change of existing processes, puts him on the alert and can make him sabotage potential plans by saying yes but doing nothing. If you come to Luke with a new idea and he says, "I am not sure if that will work,"

Easygoing Laid-Back Luke avoids using too much effort.

he may actually mean, "It might be a fine plan; however, it sounds like a lot of work, so I'd better discourage it as fast as possible!" The lucky thing about Luke is that he is laid back and friendly, so he will not make an active effort to block you from executing your idea. He may even give you some useful advice if he can do so easily. Just don't expect him to make big efforts.

Luke is social and friendly. He is often the party starter at receptions and events, so he is often the guy adding fun to the organization's culture. Try to appreciate him for that. If you spend time with him during lunch, you'll find that he has a relaxing influence on people. Don't expect too much from him in other areas, though. If you really need something from Luke, you may have to prompt him a few times before he actually delivers. If you do that consistently, he will always deliver in the end, especially if he feels that you are a nice person. Make a habit of double checking the work he delivers to you. Though Luke can be good at his work, he doesn't always pay enough attention to deliver perfect output, and he may sometimes try to cover up mistakes.

5. Fake It Until You Make It Freddy

Fake It Freddy talks a lot but says nothing of importance.

Freddy's most important skill is his faking skill. This does not mean that this type of person is never skilled. It mainly means that he will always try to make things he knows and delivers look bigger and better than they really are. He speaks a lot without saying much. Everything he says *sounds* important, but you can almost randomly take a sample from his words and replace them with "*blah, blah, blah, blah*" without losing much information. If others don't create a clear structure and objectives, Freddy can block all progress on a project by making conversations go all over the place without coming to conclusions and decisions. He tends to draw attention to himself during meetings, and he fails to notice that four out of five people in the room have started yawning, looking out the window, or text messaging while he is talking.

In principle, people like Freddy are not very damaging as long as you don't allow yourself to waste too much time taking his bluffs too seriously. You'll need to critically assess what information that he gives you is useful and what is not, and you will sometimes need to enforce a decision to move forward. You may also need to overrule Freddy when he's speaking during meetings. If you try to be too friendly, there will be a lack of focus, and meetings will take an unnecessarily long time, which can result in losing the energy of the other people in the room. Though you may have to interrupt Freddy often, he has no bad intentions. He'll accept it if you take the lead to make sure that conversations keep progressing. He may even feel that you have helped him organize his thoughts. Freddy is likely to be aware of the fact he talks too much and may even joke about it himself, so a bit of humor may be a great way of connecting to him and stopping his words from time to time. He is basically a nice and entertaining guy with good intentions that you have to take with a pinch of salt every now and then.

6. Napoleon

Napoleon is charismatic and intelligent, and while he is known to lash out at employees regularly, he is still admired. He can be dominant and unpredictable. Don't go into a meeting with him when you're unprepared. He'll see gaps in your work from miles away and will grind you down because of it. Also, do not undermine his authority in front of others if you don't have to. He'll remember it for quite some time if you do. Especially for somewhat insecure people, Napoleon can be intimidating, and that may make them nervous when they discuss business with him. Indeed, Napoleon is very hard to impress, and it can be almost impossible to change his mind; however, if you do counter him with a solid and convincing rationale, he will respect you for it.

Napoleon is very skilled and has clear vision and leadership. He can get big things done. You shouldn't expect too much friendliness, though. He rarely gives a compliment, and it can be hard to build a personal relationship with him. Napoleon is a strong people observer. He uses that to place the right people in the right places so that great things can happen, yet

The Napoleon manager: charismatic yet frightening.

sometimes he also uses it to put people under pressure, touching exactly on their weak points. He is well organized, but he can also harm efficiency and morale by changing his mind unexpectedly. If that happens, try to hear him out, though, for he is likely to have good reasons for the change of course.

It is generally not easy working with Napoleon. However, if you can find a way to make it work, you will feel that you're part of a great mission. Stay relaxed, know your stuff, and don't say yes to something that you can't or don't want to deliver.

7. Mastermind Mario

Mastermind Mario is very difficult to recognize. He is charming and intelligent, he is a good storyteller with a broad knowledge base, and he is understanding of people. He can enchant you with a combination of flattery and wisdom, yet he can also use those skills to manipulate people so that he gets

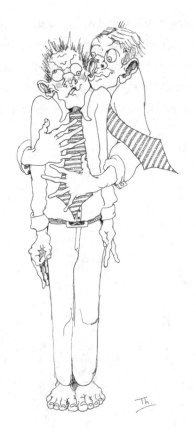

Mastermind Mario takes control of you while nobody notices.

his way. His manipulations are likely to be so subtle and focused on a specific person that most of the time they go unnoticed by other people. He is a great creative thinker, but he may be so indulgent with his own ideas that he doesn't care about feasibility. If he lures you into working on his ideas, you'll always need to be critical concerning whether what he asks from you can actually be done. However, the idea may be great.

Mario is calm, collected, warm, friendly, and thoughtful, which makes him very skilled in selling his ideas. He is very convincing in client-facing roles and tends to be forward-looking in inspiring ways. Mario does not care much about details of execution, though, so he needs the people around him to bring his ideas to life. Don't challenge his ideas in public, because he has little tolerance for that. He likes to be admired, and the illusion of his infinite wisdom may even be valuable in motivating many people in the office to do great things. Let yourself be inspired by his ideas and learn from the conversations you have with him while at the same time evaluating what he is saying critically. Before you promise to help him execute one of his ideas, take a step back to evaluate its feasibility and weigh the tasks against your other priorities. Don't just say yes out of excitement and enchantment.

8. Parasite Patricia

Parasite Patricia claims others' success at their expense.

In conversation, you will notice that Parasite Patricia likes to repeat something that you've already said—rebranded as her own. She is not particularly damaging, but it is wise not to share ideas with her before making other people aware that the ideas are yours. Once it is clear that you are the source of a great idea or project, Patricia will probably be a positive contributor to the success that you create together. Patricia is well organized, particularly when it comes to mobilizing her team or teammates.

She knows how to motivate the right people at the right moments. If Patricia is a manager, she'll be aware that her career is dependent on the success of her team, so she can be a great encouraging coach. As a team-mate, Patricia is likely to be a pleasant coworker who shows appreciation for your work and your ideas. When given the opportunity, she'll over-state her role in the success you created together, though.

Since Patricia tends to be very tactical, she often replies to questions with socially desired answers, making it hard to find out what she really thinks about sensitive or political matters. If that leads to a lack of clarity, you may sometimes need to push a little to really hear her opinion. In gen-eral, you can work with Patricia most easily if you give her a clear role that she can claim. Be aware that she may claim more if she can, but that may not always be a problem. If it isn't, let her have it. After all, she makes many invisible contributions by bringing people together and helping them be successful. So why not let her claim part of that? Consider explicitly ask-ing Patricia to share the credit with the people who deserve it. You'll find that Patricia is very skilled in creating a great stage for all of you. If there are certain people who need to know about your contribution, like your own manager and important stakeholders, consider establishing your own direct line of communication with them so that you can make sure that Patricia does not diminish your role.

9. Weakling Willy

Weakling Willy is friendly and kind, but he often looks like he is carrying a heavy burden. He tends to be either submissive or too friendly, and he almost never says no. Even though Willy always has the sincere intention of delivering what he promises, he often doesn't. He basically promises too much to too many people at the same time. To make things worse, he does not work very well under pressure. Willy continually finds himself in the position of not being able to stick to his plan, which is very stressful to him and may even result in his ending up sick at home (where he will still try to do some work). You may not always notice the pressure that Willy is under,

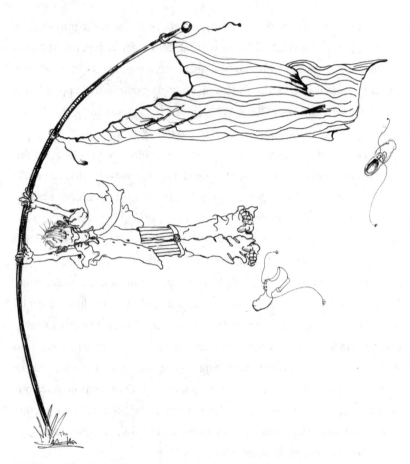

Weakling Willy changes direction with every hint of wind.

for when he is stressed, he tends to become quiet and almost invisible. If he is afraid that things are going wrong, instead of seeking help or fixing things, he panics, stops communicating, and may try to cover up his mistakes.

It is easy to put Willy under pressure to have him do things. There is no use in pushing him, though, when something needs to be delivered; he will just get more nervous and perform less well. It works better if you provide encouragement, safety, and structure. Help Willy organize his priorities. If you can, get some weight off his shoulders by helping him with some of his tasks, so that he can free up time to work on what you need from him. It also helps if you can manage to get people to leave Willy alone for some time, for instance, by encouraging him to work from home every now and then. Because he says yes so easily, there may be a steady stream of people coming to his desk and asking him for small favors. If you can divert that stream and help Willy be relaxed and focused, you may find that he is actually really good at what he does. You just need to help him focus on those things where he uniquely adds value, while others take care of the rest. Give him confirmation that he has the skills to do what he needs to. Check in with him regularly on a proactive basis, for he may get stuck on small things that you can help him overcome with some pragmatic workarounds. In general, try not to make yourself dependent on his commitment.

10. Trapped Theo

Trapped Theo undermines his efficiency as a result of high sustained stress levels.

When Trapped Theo is under a lot of stress, he doesn't seem to be himself. Feelings of pressure will undermine his efficiency, clear thinking, and decision making, as well as the relationships he has with people and his ability to cooperate with them. Basically, any person can become Trapped Theo, for anyone can do strange things when he is under sustained high pressure. If Theo does negative things that you normally would not expect him to do, it is likely that there is something structurally wrong at work, in his personal life, or maybe both at the same time. This could be a reorganization, a damaged relationship with colleagues or a manager, structural work overload, or something like the death of a loved one.

Depending on the extent to which Theo feels trapped, his personality can move in any direction. His behaviors are likely to go to extremes. He may, for instance, start involving everyone in the things he is doing, but it is also very possible that he will become quiet and stop communicating. He may become cold or unkind in the interest of preserving himself, or he may become emotionally unstable. He may start inventing new ideas and solutions to save his situation, even though those ideas may be far from realistic. Just as likely, he ends up daring almost nothing anymore. It's good to realize that Theo is going through a hard time and that he can use help and understanding to make a positive change. Don't put him under pressure, for sustained pressure is the exact reason that he is in this situation. A reset of his environment can help make sure that the same issues do not arise again too soon. In general, stay aware that under pressure, anyone can do things that she normally wouldn't.

14

THE BEST VICTORIES

In business, you will often find yourselves in situations where your objectives conflict with those of others, where you need to convince others of your view, or where you may even be in competition with them. In martial arts, if you are a truly skilled fighter, you can defeat an opponent while at the same time protecting him from harm. Being truly skilled works the same way in business. If you feel that your colleagues do not embrace your ideas, you can either keep pushing to the point where they have no choice but to accept your view or help them see how they can benefit from your ideas and give them the opportunity to be successful when they embrace those ideas. The latter approach lasts longer: always aim for the success of your project while allowing others to come out strong as well. That can be achieved only if you learn to place yourself in the shoes of others; you have to figure out what drives them and what concerns them.

> *Always aim for the success of your project while allowing others to come out strong as well.*

If you have meetings with people, make a habit of taking the first 10 or 15 minutes to figure out what they hope to get out of the meeting. This is particularly important when you are meeting with people you don't know yet. Try to assess what both their long-term and their short-term objectives are.

It is great for you to have ambition and build success, but try to do so in a way that does not harm others.

Try to find their professional goals and what results they are rewarded for, but also their personal goals. Professional and personal goals may not always be the same. For example, someone who is unhappy in his job may choose to work on a project with you mainly because you are a nice person or because your project gives him an opportunity to build his skills and visibility so that he can switch to a new job later. If you are aware of these kinds of objectives, you can help others succeed while contributing to common projects.

Personal objectives may sometimes be particularly difficult to uncover. When you are in a group meeting, a colleague is unlikely to explain to you that she is considering a career change. You might need to start a casual conversation outside of the meeting to find out these kinds of things. Some personal goals may be visible only if you read between the lines. If you are attentive, you may, for instance, discover that a certain colleague feels insecure and is being pushed around by others. You can make a big difference for such a person by just giving him a heartfelt compliment at the right moment or by acknowledging his great work in front of others. This, of course, works only if you really mean it.

The optimal mindset for fruitful cooperation can best be summarized as "win-win or no deal!" There are two sides to that statement. On the one hand, it is not healthy if you structurally enter cooperations in which you invest more than you get back. That diminishes your ability to do great things sustainably and may reduce your ability to contribute to the projects you participate in. Keep in mind that your partners will benefit if you feel an internal drive to push the joint project, so there needs to be a benefit for you personally. The same is true the other way around. You don't want to be in a position where you have to push others all the time to keep them contributing to your projects, so there needs to be a clear benefit for them if they do so. Do everything in your power to make your cooperation with people as fruitful for them as it is for you. If you cannot find sufficient common ground, it is perfectly fine to decide *not* to cooperate, or at least not now on that specific topic. You'll be better off in the long run if you find others who get (or see) more benefit from cooperation on that topic. At the same time, you'll prevent harming a relationship by the structural friction that can come from the unbalance of working on a project that is not beneficial to both sides.

If you have the misfortune of finding yourself in a situation involving a serious professional conflict, always strive to find the common ground that is a starting point for negotiation. No matter how far apart the two

> *No matter how far apart the two sides in a conflict seem to be, if you dig deep enough, you will always be able to find some form of common ground.*

sides in a conflict seem to be, if you dig deep enough, you will always be able to find some form of common ground. Even in wars, common ground can be found. Associations involved in peace negotiations often use the need for all sides to prevent unnecessary collateral damage among children in their own countries as a door opener. The will to protect your spouse is such a powerful force that it can open up conversations in situations where a war seems to have eliminated all possibilities of ever coming together. The artist Sting sings about this in his beautiful song "Russians" using the words "I hope the Russians love their children too." If you find one opening that allows you to have a conversation, you will most likely find another, and then still another after that. Strive to allow all players to come out of negotiations and conflicts as strong as possible. The best win is when your opponent does not feel defeated.

> *The best win is when your opponent does not feel defeated.*

In a competitive situation, there can generally be only one winner, yet you always have the choice of how you shape your route toward victory (or loss). You can choose to talk others down and attack their weaknesses, or you can choose to trust in your own skill and focus on building on your own strengths and creating the best possible output you have in you. Even competition doesn't need to be a win-lose game. The best sports matches are always those in which both players or teams have the courage to harness everything they have in them to create a stunning match for the audience. If both sides refrain from the temptation to play from a negative defensive angle, they will both rise to the occasion and feel the thrill of the competition, and both will be winners from the experience. In sports, you need strong opponents to sharpen your skills. This is also true in business, so let yourself be inspired by people, organizations, and companies that compete with you. I remember reading the

Do everything in your power to make your cooperation with people as fruitful for them as it is for you: "win-win, or no deal" is the spirit.

life story of a great Japanese warrior called Musashi. Musashi is known as one of the greatest samurai that ever lived. He was renowned for his skill of fighting with two swords. By a conservative estimate, Musashi fought more than 60 duels and was never defeated. At some point late in his career as a warrior, he defeated Sasaki Kojiro, known as "The Demon of the Western Provinces," who was his strongest opponent. The fight was an epic battle that Musashi allegedly fought with a wooden sword that he had personally carved from an oar used on the boat that carried him to the island where the fight took place. Looking at the dead body of his opponent after the duel, Musashi took some time to reflect and thank his opponent for having been so strong and having challenged his skills. With a wave of admiration and respect, he realized that he would never meet an opponent like him again.

> *In sports, you need strong opponents to sharpen your skills. This is also true in business, so let yourself be inspired by people, organizations, and companies that compete with you.*

People in business tend to work from one of two mindsets. Either they see business as competition or even a form of waging war, or they see business as a journey in which you build great work with great people. People who look at business as if it were war tend to distrust people until proven otherwise; they tend to be controlling and ask questions to pick holes in people's work. They monitor risks and gather people around them who will do exactly what they want them to do. People who see business as building great work with great people trust people until proven otherwise and support an environment in which people can express their ideas. They ask questions to expand and sharpen those ideas. They scan their environment for opportunities and protect those opportunities from risks. They gather people around them because of their unique skills and creative thinking, people who can do things that they can't do themselves and that they may never think of doing. I hope this book inspires you to walk that second route, so you can help me prove that companies and organizations can build great results by creating a joyful and harmonious work environment.

15

BALANCE POWER
WITH RESPONSIBILITY

Since there are people in any company who resist change, tactics for persuading them are always important. However, as you get more skilled in these tactics, you risk losing yourself in tactical behavior to the point where it can be considered office politics. Office politics are generally harmful for long-term company success and to office culture. The line between useful but harmless tactics and office politics can be very thin sometimes, so how do you walk that line without crossing over to the wrong side?

Beware that useful tactics do not become harmful office politics.

First of all, it is important for you to realize in more detail when and why tactics serve an important purpose, so let's dive a bit deeper into that. As you grow into more senior jobs, there are more complexities, more stakeholders, more pressures, and fewer straightforward answers. The acceleration of change has required many traditional companies to fundamentally transform themselves, and in such transformations, almost no one has a full overview of what needs to be done. In the process of change, many professionals may need to acquire new skills. And when people can't adapt their skills or when change requires the company to work with fewer resources, people may need to be fired. Who is to tell you what the optimal choices are when you are analyzing fast and complex changing trends? If the company doesn't fire ten people today, it may need to fire a hundred people next year or a thousand people ten years from now.

If the answers to the questions you are facing are not straightforward, and at the same time people feel that they are risking potential loss, they are more likely to feel threatened. Because of that, people may challenge the decisions that are being made. In its mildest form, that will result in people asking for clarification of the reasoning behind your decisions. Those questions may often be completely justifiable. In its worst form, people will fight the change with every means available to them. They may start attacking individuals rather than the perspectives they represent, and they may try to persuade other people to join them in battle. A common but less noticeable form of sabotaging is work avoidance or focusing only on today's issues. In the descriptions of 10 office personalities in Chapter 13, you could see that people have their own ways and reasons for blocking things that they don't want to have happen. For companies to keep moving and developing at the required pace, enough supporters need to make an effort to make sure that people don't slip back into their regular ways of doing things or start doing damaging things to the company for their own personal reasons. Getting a group of people to adjust their ways of working is not just a matter of telling them what to do. The group needs to be guided through the process of change on a day-to-day basis. This is not a task just for senior managers. As many people as possible should support that process of change at all levels of the organization.

That means that in many cases, there will be a role for you too, and you'll need the right tactical skills to help guide the company through the change.

In general, people will resist change if they think that their loss will be greater than the benefit of the change. Such a loss can be as simple as the fear of getting a heavier workload as a result of the change or the fear of becoming redundant. If you try to mobilize people around a new project, idea, or decision but you fail to understand the personal losses that people may experience, you'll feel like you're fighting a ghost. People may nod yes when you speak to them, but they are likely to keep slipping back to their default behaviors without you fully understanding why. Many people are afraid of communicating their worries, and some may even consciously but silently try to sabotage what you are trying to do; as a result, they may not always be open and may not let you see their underlying motives. If you have the feeling that this is what's happening, go back to the drawing board and try to understand what people may fear losing or what they are gaining by keeping things as they are. Some potential losses may be small enough to overcome. Other potential losses may be so important that they really need to be avoided in order to win people's support. Try to understand people's position within the wider company and within their teams, try to see the pressures they are under, and you'll get a feeling for what is driving their resistance.

> *In general, people will resist change if they think that their loss will be greater than the benefit of the change.*

See if you can stretch people's mindsets to look beyond the now and their individual positions. Ideally, you can make people see an advantage from the change that is bigger than what they fear losing. That may mean that you need to invest in making sure that there is backup for risks, for instance, by having a strong alignment with their superiors and by getting the right influencers on board. If you have the right support, you can give people the safety they need to take responsibility and face the potential risks. Sometimes you need to get people to see that change is inevitable and that fighting it is harmful in the long run. The most common example here is consumers shifting their purchases to the Internet, which affects many types of businesses. You can choose to fight such developments or you can join them. Either way, the change is happening, so it is a matter of choosing between the short-term pain of changing and the painful long-term consequences of *not* changing. For many companies, the shift toward digital is still ongoing. If you are a digital thinker, you can help prevent companies from having a "Kodak moment."

> *For many companies, the shift toward digital is still ongoing. If you are a digital thinker, you can help prevent companies from having a "Kodak moment."*

Kodak was a global leader in photographic equipment and services for many years. In 1976, Kodak commanded 90 percent of film sales in the United States and 85 percent of camera sales, according to a 2005 case study from Harvard Business School. However, Kodak missed the shift to digital photography. Kodak was the inventor of digital photography; however, the company failed to pursue it to avoid the risk of disrupting its existing business, thus leaving room for competing companies to walk away with the idea and make it a success. Kodak filed for bankruptcy protection in 2012. It received funding and was able to continue as a severely slimmed down version of what it had once been, completely stopping the making of digital cameras. Examples like Kodak are illustrative of the consequences for companies that fail to move toward digitizing along with their customers.

With your digital mindset, you are in a great position to show your colleagues how the Internet affects their business. You can paint the most lively picture to help people see the benefits of becoming more digital-savvy. You *are* the urgency for change, so they can see it in you. Hence, if you connect to your colleagues in the right way and understand their motives, your potential for building strong persuasive powers on the topic of digital change is enormous. In some cases, though, you'll need to accept that there will be casualties. Some people will always be troublemakers, and some people are in an unfortunate position that can't be changed. That is just the nature of being in a world that is never static.

When you are working with many people on a big project in a complex environment, even if everyone fully and sincerely cooperates, their collective behavior may be so hard to manage that it creates a mess, undermining the success of the project. For instance, when you ask people for feedback, each individual may give it, yet their separate pieces of input may be completely conflicting. Some people may come in late in the process with feedback that makes hours of prior work done by others completely irrelevant, not because they wanted to be annoying, but just because they weren't aware of all the steps that had already been taken.

> *When you are working with many people on a big project in a complex environment, even if everyone fully and sincerely cooperates, their collective behavior may be so hard to manage that it creates a mess, undermining the success of the project.*

An example from my own experience is the creation of a questionnaire for the purpose of market research. Such a questionnaire needs to have a clear scope because the number of questions you can ask one respondent is limited. If the questionnaire is too long or if the questions lack a coherent structure, respondents' willingness or ability to give accurate answers is reduced. If that happens, the resulting data are flawed, leading to decision making based on the wrong information. If you ask a group of 10 colleagues to give you feedback on the content of a questionnaire, each of them will give you input coming from different angles and perspectives. They will all push to have certain questions included because they want to have certain topics covered. If you accept all their suggestions and feedback, the questionnaire will become a complete mess, lacking a structure and being far too extensive. Many researchers lack the tactical skills to manage these conversations and to enforce trade-offs that allow the inclusion of as much feedback as possible without interfering with the central objective of the research. As a result, a lot of research is based on messy questionnaires, resulting in flawed data and decisions. At the other end of the spectrum is research that has not been aligned well with all stakeholders and therefore lacks relevance. Sometimes you need to listen to people, and sometimes there are good reasons for you to cast their opinions or wishes aside. Finding that balance is often hard and requires you to manage all stakeholders in tactical ways. The same tactical skills are needed to help guide an organization through change.

Stakeholder management is the art of balance: a balance between listening and directing, between tactics and sincere openness.

Creating a questionnaire is a relatively easy task involving a relatively small group of people compared to the tasks that most senior professionals face when they are trying to transform their organizations. The most complex example of transformation is probably a government running a country or making decisions about issues like the global financial crisis. Economists, statisticians, and leaders have warned for many years that countries' rates of spending would eventually not be sustainable and that severe budget cuts were needed. However, a majority of the population is not capable of seeing the consequences of their actions if those consequences are 10 or more years ahead. As a result, it is basically impossible to get voters to agree to severe sacrifices in terms of their current standard of living to deal with a problem that they do not yet see coming. In the case of some environmental issues, we might be even talking about the quality of life for generations to come. How do you convince a majority of people that the current rate of using energy is not sustainable if they may not see the negative consequences within their lifetime or even that of their children? It is only now, with the implications of the financial crisis becoming clear, that voters in some countries are starting to accept budget cuts or amendments of rules and laws. Meanwhile, a lot of the damage has already been done, and as a result, economies often find themselves running into catastrophes, like a big cruise ship that's about to hit an iceberg minutes ahead.

People's collective behavior can make organizations seem like monster machines that are hard to steer. In the end we will get there, though, just as most ships reach their destination. Most tasks carried out by professionals will be at a level of complexity somewhere between the two extremes of building a questionnaire for the purpose of market research and solving global governmental issues. All professional work will therefore suffer to some extent from the impossibility of all individuals foreseeing all consequences, and hence it is inevitable that a certain amount of tactics will always be needed to keep projects from dying through either compromise or chaos. So there are clearly many useful elements in displaying the right tactical behavior at the right moment. But where do tactics end and bad habits begin? When do tactics become harmful office politics?

People's collective behavior can make organizations seem like monster machines that are hard to steer.

It is hard to say exactly, because it varies from case to case. Is Opportunistic Olivia being egotistic when she gets people to work on her goals, or is she just doing what is necessary to make her project a success? Is Collateral Damage Danny really unnecessarily hard and impersonal, or is he doing what is needed to keep your organization financially healthy in the long run? Sometimes soft doctors make dirty wounds. Mastermind Mario enchants us by faking his infinite knowledge, but sometimes we just want and need to be enchanted to snap us out of our limited thinking. Given the thin line between damaging political behavior and necessary tactics, all professionals need to reflect from time to time on their own behavior. Are the things you are doing still focused on the objectives, rather than, for instance, just making yourself look good or making someone else look bad? Are the sacrifices you make still in balance with the objectives that they aim to facilitate? Are you still making the right ethical trade-offs? I ask myself these kinds of questions every day.

> *Given the thin line between damaging political behavior and necessary tactics, all professionals need to reflect from time to time on their own behavior.*

Particularly in the early days of my career, I often felt that I was under pressure. That could lead to negative feelings about top-down decisions made in the organization when those decisions created extra work for me that I felt was useless. If I felt that I was ill informed about a particular decision, that was highly frustrating to me. Through experience, I have learned how tough and complex the decisions that senior leaders need to make are. These are decisions that do not have a right or a wrong answer—just trade-offs. I have come to understand how hard it can be to make everyone aware of what decisions have been made, what trade-offs have been made, and why. As a result, I have learned not to let my peace of mind be disturbed by top-down changes that are enforced in the organization. I have learned to ask in a straightforward way why decisions have been made, what the implications are, and how I can contribute to make the transfer to a new situation a success. That way I keep my peace of mind so that I can continue building value without feeling a grudge or engaging in negative behavior.

I have also had moments where I was so convinced of the importance of my long-term goals and priorities that I felt it was not important for me to attend weekly internal meetings that sometimes discussed topics that were repetitive in nature. I started to consider those meetings a waste of time, and since I was performing very well, I felt that I could skip them once in a while. I forgot, though, that when you move higher in the hierarchy, you start to become a role model for others. And if the role models can't stick to organization or team policy, then why should the rest of the employees do so? I have learned to follow company rules and fit into company structures better over time. I have learned to help make weekly meetings more useful for everyone by setting the agenda and sharing my ideas or experiences. Of course, there is a balance here. A good organization hires great professionals first of all for their creativity, drive, and proactivity. You don't get those by just following corporate guidelines. Alignment with corporate guidelines still remains important, though, and I felt that I could make much more of an effort than I had once done to align my goals and work methods with those of the company.

Finally, I have become more skilled over time in convincing people that they should make contributions to my projects and ideas. If I have a request of a colleague or other stakeholder, I am very aware that the way I frame that request determines whether or not the person will decide to contribute. The skill of pitching your ideas is in general an important one if you are going to build great things. I have learned to be creative in showing people their own stake in being part of my projects, and therefore many people are happy to work with me. I have often wondered, though: When does this tactic become a way of luring people into helping? It's hard to say exactly. I have tried to create guidelines for myself to keep me on the fair side. First of all, I approach people with my request only if I truly believe it will also be of value to them. I try to inform people as transparently as possible so that they know exactly what they are saying yes to; if I have a request, they'll know exactly how much will be asked of them. Then if they choose to work with me, I make sure that they are not disappointed and that they are part of the success. I always make an effort to give back at least what I receive in terms of effort or value. I do so mostly by sharing knowledge, helping colleagues be successful, and doing specific favors as soon as possible if they arise. How do you quantify, though, whether what you are giving back to people equals what they are giving to you? This is just not always clear.

I'd like to encourage you to reflect on your behavior in similar ways and train yourself to stay on the fair side. Look at yourself in the mirror every day and ask yourself, "Am I still doing the right thing, or am I crossing the line into political behavior?" The awareness exercise in Chapter 4 will help you check whether you are still focusing on the right objectives for yourself and for the company. You can then reflect on whether you are still working on the right things in the right ways. Don't judge yourself for not being perfect. Just focus on your good intentions. If you find yourself displaying any negative behaviors, ask yourself what triggered them. Do you still love the work you do? Do you feel that you are treated with respect? Are you feeling appreciated and rewarded? Which environmental factors made you do things that you do not want to see yourself doing? In Chapter 9 I mentioned that there are three ways to cope with problems crossing your path: change it, accept it, or leave. If you fail to choose among these three options when you are facing problems, that increases the risk that you'll start displaying political behavior or other negative behavior because you feel that you are trapped in something that structurally makes you unhappy, frustrated, or angry. Take responsibility for your job happiness. It is too important not to do that. You are a better person if you feel good while you are spending your time at work. That will help you always use your tactical powers in ethical and responsible ways.

> *Take responsibility for your job happiness. It is too important not to do that. You are a better person if you feel good while you are spending your time at work.*

PART V

KEEP YOUR ASPIRATIONS AND WORK PLEASURE ALIVE

16

SHOOT FOR THE MOON

Moonshots are projects that offer your company and the world a true leap forward. You're not just optimizing what is already there by a few percent every year but instead launching a new idea that brings what are called "10X improvements," making things 10 times better. Digital thinkers are in a key position to deliver on moonshot thinking, but only if they allow themselves to be free of existing standards and if they can mobilize other colleagues to embrace their thinking. Companies that dedicate part of their resources to moonshots are ready for any type of change and will be able to stay alive and fresh over decades.

> *Companies that dedicate part of their resources to moonshots are ready for any type of change and will be able to stay alive and fresh over decades.*

Moonshots in the context of technological development were described by Astro Teller of Google in a *Wired* article. He oversees the Google X team, which works on sci-fi projects like self-driving cars and Google Glass. These projects aim to deal with issues by making products not a few percent better, but instead *10* times better or even more. If you shoot for 10 times better and make it only 80 percent of the way, you have still come further then when you fully succeed in improving something by 10 percent. If you are shooting for a 10 percent improvement, a large part of your thinking will be limited to the things you already know and can do. If you "shoot for the moon," you'll aim for radical change and seek for fundamentally new knowledge and skills. Moonshots are not limited to technology but can, for instance, also be social in nature, so the concept can apply to any company you work for.

Shoot for the moon by setting meaningful and audacious goals.

Moonshot thinking, as explained by Astro Teller, starts with a big problem: something huge, long-existing, and on a global scale. Next, it involves a radical solution, one that would actually solve the problem if it existed. Finally, there needs to be some kind of evidence that the proposed solution is not quite as crazy as it first seems.

For example, all three elements are true for the idea of making digital thinkers the key drivers for keeping companies future-ready as I will explain in the next paragraphs.

ADAPTATION OF BIG ESTABLISHED COMPANIES AND ORGANIZATIONS IS A PERPETUAL PROBLEM

The problem of companies becoming slower to adapt to their environment as they become more established and bigger has always existed. It is *not* a new problem that relates only to the digital world, and it happens to companies all over the world. It is for this exact reason that every major change or technical breakthrough is an opportunity for new young companies to enter existing markets by being faster than the companies that have already invested in older techniques and methods. Younger generations have always been the ones to embrace new developments and ideas first, and they are likely to keep doing that. Right now it is gen Y that offers us lots of digital thinkers who can help organizations be future-ready, but there will be many more generations to come that can do so in the decades ahead of us.

THE RADICAL SOLUTION: A TWO-WAY MENTORSHIP BETWEEN DIGITAL THINKERS AND SENIOR LEADERS

The radical solution is to create an ongoing two-way mentorship program linking our most talented digital thinkers to senior leaders at all levels and in all areas of the company. Make at least one and preferably multiple digital thinkers part of a company's advisory board or management team, and link a digital thinker to every senior manager in the company. That would offer digital thinkers the opportunity to bring fresh ideas to the surface at all levels and in all areas of the organization, while senior managers can help them see the balance involving other strategic trade-offs that need to be made.

Imagine that you as a digital thinker could sit in the meetings where your senior managers discuss company strategy. You could represent the new world in those meetings and clarify what you see, so that the leaders can discuss what that means for strategy. You could help in making a strong case for investment in future readiness that requires inevitable trade-offs against existing business. You could urge the company to keep investing in moonshots, thereby helping to prevent it from slipping back into its default tactics over and over again, doing what made it successful in previous years until the point where it is too late to embrace change. At the same time, you would get direct feedback on your ideas from the senior managers in the meeting. They could help you see how various goals in the company are related to one another and affect one another, and hence they could help you see your ideas in a realistic context. If your new ideas are strong enough, senior managers can help you mobilize groups of people to embrace and drive these ideas until they become reality. Creating a two-way mentorship like this is a relatively small and feasible step that can have profound impact: the company will attract, retain, and develop more talented digital thinkers, and the company strategy will keep focusing on future readiness.

THE DIGITAL AGE FORCES COMPANIES TO MAKE A STEP CHANGE

The evidence available to illustrate that this idea is not entirely crazy comes from the consequences of the increased transparency and rate of change fueled by the emergence of the Internet and by new technological developments. As I have explained, those have put a huge amount of pressure on companies to redefine their adaptive skills. I explained in Chapter 2 how transparency increases the pressure on companies to be best in class relative to the competition, while the rate of change increases the pressure to continue to be the best by establishing a continuous flow of innovation that increases in speed over time. I explained how CEOs are more ready than ever to listen to digital thinkers like you. They already invite experts over for occasional events to inspire them and teach them about the latest digital developments. So why not do this on a structural basis, utilizing the most talented digital natives who already work inside the company? A network of digital thinkers working for the company and distributed throughout all levels and all areas of the company will be in a much better position to be a continuous force for change than a group of external speakers, and thus they will have a much bigger and more sustainable impact—the exact impact needed to achieve 10X improvements.

So there is an open mindset among the senior management, there are concrete actions that can be taken, and there is the commercial drive to utilize the power of gen Y and all other digital thinkers to keep companies future-ready. All the ingredients are there now. With this combination of factors, it can be done. Companies and professionals that are not willing to rid themselves of old patterns are likely to decrease in number fast. It is just a matter of time.

Companies and professionals that are not willing to rid themselves of old patterns are likely to decrease in number fast. It is just a matter of time.

The idea of a two-way mentoring program fits the nonhierarchical mindset of gen Y professionals while acknowledging that senior managers have important experience that gen Y professionals can and should benefit from. It acknowledges the power of a fresh new idea, regardless of where that idea comes from, while ensuring that such an idea finds alignment with the right people and existing activities at the right moments. It is the optimal combination of maturity and juvenile freshness that can make great things happen. The company culture is likely to benefit a lot, it will be easier for the company to attract and retain young talent, and consumers and clients will keep getting the latest and greatest products and services from the organizations they already know and trust.

17

NAÏVETÉ: THE SOURCE OF FUNDAMENTAL INNOVATION

Many young people enter their working lives with what you could call naïve aspirations. They want to create a better world and leave a big impression. Many professionals lose these aspirations over time, and the word *naïveté* has come to have a negative connotation in the minds of many senior professionals. But naïveté can also be a blessing and a power. It is the skill of asking questions without assuming that you know the answers and looking at problems with a fresh and clear mind. Naïveté is the skill of looking at people, ideas, and solutions free of prejudice. It is the source of all fundamental innovation, the type of innovation that triggers moonshots.

When they start their careers, many young professionals go through a few years of turbulence before they understand the unwritten rules of their offices. Some may start with an attitude that is overcourageous; they challenge ideas all over the place, and by doing so, bump into resistance and risk being rejected by colleagues. Others may feel the urge to be as cooperative as possible and to help out wherever they can. Those youngsters may find themselves in situations where they are overloaded with and doing "dirty" jobs that other people don't want to do. Some young professionals may not immediately have the courage to speak up; they may feel that their thoughts are not smart or important enough to be heard. These

Many people enter their working lives with big aspirations to make things different. Some people may call this naïveté; however, it is the source of all innovation—the skill to ask fresh questions and to aspire to big things.

people may find themselves in situations where their work and skills are not valued and rewarded appropriately, and they may get stuck in jobs that do not inspire them to make the maximum use of their talents.

In the process of adapting to work life, part of the naïveté of our young professionals is often lost, and as a result, their professional lives start to focus on incremental thinking instead of moonshots. Incremental thinking is very common in companies. It means that people do approximately what they did before, with a few minor changes. This happens a lot because it's natural for people to want to work on things that they know aren't going to fail. Incremental thinking is an easy way of getting your plans accepted and your efforts appreciated by the majority, since it fits with what people know and what has been proven to work in the past. That makes incremental thinking a relatively safe investment of time and money. There is no bigger waste, however, than missing an opportunity to make a fundamental difference. Hence, there is no bigger waste than depriving professionals of their naïveté. Organizations need to encourage "crazy" and "naïve" thinking. Digital thinkers need to feel empowered to capture what they see and share it with their colleagues.

The art is combining your naïveté with the right level of mature assertiveness. A certain amount of assertiveness is generally needed to get others to hear what you have to say, and people sometimes seem to think that naïveté conflicts with assertiveness. Assertiveness is often mistakenly seen as having the strength to *push* others to hear what you have to say. However, I look at assertiveness as the skill of *helping* others to hear what you have to say. From that angle, naïveté and assertiveness supplement each other seamlessly. Naïveté helps you look at the world with juvenile freshness and helps you visualize what your ideas can develop into, without taking existing knowledge and skills as a limiting starting point. If you can develop excitement about your thoughts and can simultaneously see what value it would bring to others if they could see what you see, you will feel a natural urge to share your thoughts with people in a way that makes sense to them. You will make an effort to rephrase what is in your head over and over again until people can grasp what *you* see and can relate that to what *they* are seeing. If you look at assertiveness in that way, it is basically the skill of connecting to people, understanding their perspectives, and then making your perspectives meaningful to them.

> *Naïveté helps you look at the world with juvenile freshness and helps you visualize what your ideas can develop into, without taking existing knowledge and skills as a limiting starting point.*

The word *integrity* combines both elements. It includes the will to observe things as they really are and to explore ideas without harming them with prejudice or fear of what is new or different. At the same time, it includes a longing to connect to people and to cooperate with them. It adds the element of exploring ideas coming from any person and trying to see how ideas from different people match or supplement one another. Integrity is the source of all sustainable success in our digital twenty-first century because it is the basis for the cooperation that is needed to deal with the transparency and rate of change fueled by the emergence of the Internet. We can't afford to lose the great ideas in our organizations anymore. We also can't afford to lose the people who produce those ideas, whether because they adapt themselves too much or because they leave our organizations. We need to connect those people and their ideas to all the other people in the organization so that every idea has a realistic opportunity of becoming reality.

My message to any professional is this: don't let yourself be numbed if your ideas do not resonate with colleagues. Consider it as a challenge to develop your ideas further and to formulate them in ways that resonate with the people around you. Actively work to build connections between your ideas and those of other people. Both overlaps and differences in ideas can be useful. Overlaps mean that you have found people who are thinking in similar directions, which means that they are potential supporters. Differences in ideas may offer opportunities to extend the scope of what you are working on, or they may expose a weakness in your ideas and help you to overcome that weakness. As you grow and build healthy professional relationships while working with integrity to make your own and other people's ideas reality, you will attract people with a similar mindset. You'll create an environment that gives you the energy to get up and go to work every morning. You will increasingly receive appreciation for your contribution to creating a great working culture, for that same energy also helps others to get out of bed. Don't get discouraged by any bumps in the road. Keep asking "stupid" questions, and keep coming up with "dumb" ideas and listening to those of others. Shoot for the moon and you'll achieve a lot, even if you make it only 80 percent of the way.

Keep asking "stupid" questions, and keep coming up with "dumb" ideas and listening to those of others.

BE THE "ALWAYS ON" INNOVATION ENGINE

One aspect of innovation that I believe is often overlooked is the fact that it is hard work. Innovation is often linked to having a great idea, and having a great idea tends to be interpreted as a sudden insight, like the typical lightbulb popping up inside the thought cloud of comic book characters who have the most brilliant idea ever. In my experience, idea generation is mostly a process of evangelization, adaptation, and alignment in which it may take a long time before you reach the point where an idea is clear, accepted, and feasible. The initial version of an idea may be a sudden insight, yet many steps are often needed to extend and refine that rudimentary insight, just as a rough diamond needs to be polished.

> *The initial version of an idea may be a sudden insight, yet many steps are often needed to extend and refine that rudimentary insight, just as a rough diamond needs to be polished.*

If you have an idea, you'll need to talk to a lot of people, both inside and outside the company, to test how well it resonates, how useful it is, and how feasible it is. Those conversations will lead to adaptations and even more conversations that will potentially take the idea in new directions. At some point in the process, you may start to translate the idea into conceptual versions of the product or service you are aiming for. That concept creation can help you refine the idea even further, and that kind of refinement can keep happening throughout all stages of development, even after the actual launch of a product or service.

If you have the expectation that the earliest version of your idea should be a ready-to-go product or service, you may end up waiting for that great idea for the rest of your life. You also may think that you have that great idea, while others may need a lot more elaboration to see the full potential of your idea or to believe that it can be done at all. They may see objections that you don't see, while at the same time they have a less clear picture of what the idea can become once it is fully implemented.

Others may not always see the same value in your ideas as you do, and they may find that they need to make trade-offs when embracing the idea.

That mismatch in perception leads to a different way of weighing the benefits versus the costs of embracing the idea. Based on that weighing, others might not be anywhere near as enthusiastic about it as you are.

Innovation is the art of bringing the right people and skills together at the right moment and getting them to build on one another's strengths. Some people may add thoughts to the initial idea, while others help bring it to life. Steve Jobs became famous for bringing creative and technical people together to build attractive products with a perfect user experience utilizing cutting-edge techniques. In most cases, you will also need strategic and commercially thinking people to give your ideas that extra edge that will result in a product that is not only great but also commercially successful for the company. Commercial success helps to attract even more great people so that more great products can be created. Steve Jobs was exceptional in combining his creative insights with a great nose for commercial opportunity and for bringing in the right partners. You rarely find all these skills in one single person, though, so in most cases you'll need to find them in multiple people and get those people to cooperate.

Innovation is the art of bringing the right people and skills together at the right moment and getting them to build on one another's strengths.

The model in the illustration on the following page describes how you can drive your idea from a rough diamond toward a full-fledged and optimized product or service while getting the right people on board. It's a process of iteration in which you start off with a basic idea that you pitch to the people around you. In many cases, in the beginning you'll find more people who will raise objections to the idea than people who immediately see its full value. Those who already see the full value in the earliest stage could be called the "early innovators." They can help you expand your idea into a concept that accurately describes what the product or service will be, and they can also help by evangelizing your concept to get more good people on board, the early adopters. The early adopters may raise objections that you and your innovators did not think of, given your enthusiastic mindset. These objections function as a feasibility check on the conceptual idea and can help create a first proof of concept or prototype, which is a version of the product or service that proves that the idea really works and that the objections can be overcome. The earlier you can get a working concept or prototype, the easier it will be to get people on board. Many people find it hard to visualize what an idea can be if it is not yet alive. A proof of concept or prototype helps them see the potential benefits more clearly. Offering a working concept or prototype also reduces their perception of the risks involved. If the balance between the perceived benefits

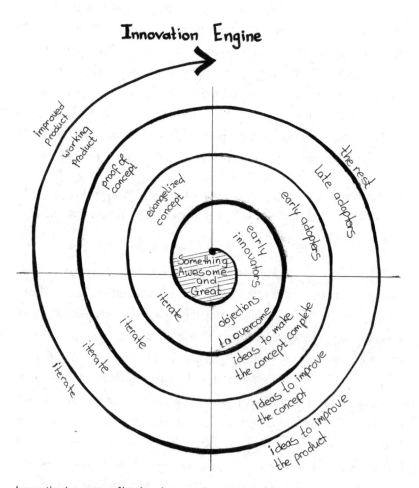

Innovation is a matter of hard work, evangelizing your ideas, getting people on board, and iterating based on their feedback.

and risks shifts enough, you'll be able to get late adopters on board to work on the final stage of making the product or service ready to be tested, then optimized and launched. In each stage of the innovation cycle, try to talk to people both in and outside the company. Talking to people outside the company is often done through qualitative and quantitative research among the potential audience for the idea or product worked on.

> *The earlier you can get a working concept or prototype, the easier it will be to get people on board. Many people find it hard to visualize what an idea can be if it is not yet alive.*

Google is known for launching its products with a beta label and keeping them like that for quite some time. This way of working fits the mindset of "launch and iterate" that Google has when it comes to innovation. Rather than sitting back in a lab waiting until the product is perfect, Google aims to get a product to market in the shortest possible time, then keeps optimizing it based on user feedback. Of course, that may not work exactly the same way for physical products like a car, a television, or a chair. For those kinds of products, optimization can't be done in real time while people are using the product, but even for them, there is a cycle of optimization after product launch. Future versions of products tend to be based on consumer feedback on earlier versions, and if there are glaring limitations to a launched product, that often results in the quickest possible launch of a new and optimized version of the product.

So be aware that almost any idea needs to go through an intensive process of iteration, and someone needs to drive that process to prevent the idea from dying. *Momentum* is a crucial ingredient in keeping that process going. Ideally, every time you speak to people about your project, you should be able to show them that you have made some progress. Every little piece of progress you made is a building block in proving that the concept can work and be successful. If you systematically keep making small steps forward with the right cadence, it will make your project feel like an inevitable movement. If you can create that spirit for your innovation, more people will want to join and support you over time. In the beginning, your support may grow slowly and the steps may be small, but if you keep making progress and building support at all levels of the organization, your project will grow in importance, and as it does, people will start feeling more urgency to help keep it moving forward. At some point, that urgency may become so great that suddenly all supporters mobilize to generate the final big bang needed to make the launch of the project the biggest success it can be. You'll find that everything becomes fluid under pressure: if people experience the right amount of urgency and the deadline is there, many things that were hard to arrange in the early stages of the innovation can suddenly be arranged within days or minutes. It is just a matter of consistency, persistence, keeping the right vibe in, and attracting the right people.

> *If you systematically keep making small steps forward with the right cadence, it will make your project feel like an inevitable movement.*

Finally, one more important ingredient for the mindset required to be a driver of innovation is summed up in the saying "It's better to ask for forgiveness than for permission." Innovation is inevitably connected to taking risks. There is always a risk that you will spend time mobilizing people to support an idea that ends in failure. Some people are averse to that kind of risk, so if you ask people for permission to proceed with your idea, you may not get it, even if the idea is great. If you wait for permission too much, you'll never do groundbreaking things. Listening to the objections that people raise will help you make sure that the risks you take are calculated risks, but don't expect that you can fully eliminate every aspect of risk.

> *Make sure that the risks you take are calculated risks, but don't expect that you can fully eliminate every aspect of risk.*

If you believe that your idea is valuable, get as many stakeholders on board as you can, embed their ideas wherever possible, be transparent about both potential risks and potential benefits, do whatever is in your power to make the project a success, and take responsibility for the outcome, whatever it is. You should always be able to explain how you made informed decisions, how you assessed the balance of risk versus potential benefit, and how you sought alignment wherever possible. Even if the project fails, if you worked with the right mindset and established the right alignment, people will respect you for it. Even a project that fails can give fulfillment, because you'll know that you gave it the shot it deserved. And, of course, if the project is a success, you and all the people who worked on it will share the glory. Don't forget to celebrate this together, for success is never a given.

19

ENJOY THE JOURNEY AND
DEFINE YOUR OWN GREATNESS

However inspiring it may be, the concept of moonshots can also have a discouraging element to it. Particularly when you're in a junior position, you may not always be able to work on the big things that will change the world or even the company. Many professionals face moments where they hear the CEO give an inspiring speech, only to be met after the speech with a big pile of annoying tasks. How do you make moonshot thinking relevant for all types of work at all job levels? By defining your own personal moonshots, big and small, that are fully tailored to your own wishes. A moonshot can be anything you want it to be, and it works best if you create a lot of them: some very close, some a bit farther away, and some that you aren't even sure are possible.

You can have a goal of becoming a wanted speaker or a CEO, while at the same time having the goal of achieving the first working week in which you were able to refrain from working too many late nights. You can aspire to become a millionaire while at the same time having the goal of stating your opinion in a meeting for the first time. Having different layers of objectives that are important to you keeps you going by both giving you long-term aspirations and offering short-term successful milestone moments.

Having different layers of objectives that are important to you keeps you going by both giving you long-term aspirations and offering short-term successful milestone moments.

I believe Nike got the messaging exactly right with its campaign called "Find your greatness." One commercial in that campaign features Nathan, a 12-year-old boy from London who weighs 200 pounds. Nathan is running on a desolate road, all on his own. The running he is doing is actually closer to walking, and he is clearly having a difficult time, sweating and breathing heavily despite his slow pace. But he is doing it, and that is the only thing that matters. Meanwhile the voice in the commercial says:

> Greatness. It's just something we made up. Somehow we've come to believe that greatness is a gift reserved for a chosen few, for prodigies, for superstars, and the rest of us can only stand by watching. You can forget that. Greatness is not some rare DNA strand. It's not some precious thing. Greatness is no more unique to us than breathing. We're all capable of it. All of us.

It is a great, award-winning commercial that is worth looking up on YouTube. Many articles were written about the campaign. Some people felt that it was inspiring, while others felt that it was mocking fat people. The only thing that matters, though, is what Nathan feels. Nathan himself reported that shooting the commercial had inspired him to go to the gym, and he felt good about it. He wrote on Facebook afterward:

> Went to the gym for the first day! It was fun! Hard though, but that just means its working, RIGHT?
>
> —*Nathan Sorrell*

I'd say the message here is that you need to feel what drives you and pick your own milestones based on that. Going to the gym for the first time may not sound like a big deal if you do it several times a week, and we don't know whether Nathan was able to keep at it, yet the fact that he felt good about himself at that moment is what matters. It's precisely these small moments that can help you keep going over and over again. They give you the energy to keep trying. Use your bigger goals and moonshots to give you a sense of your long-term direction, but also give yourself many small goals so that you know what to focus on now and so that you have successes to look forward to. The most important criterion for selecting any goal is the fact that it drives *you*. Of course you need to align your goals with your surroundings at work, but if a goal doesn't drive you, it is unlikely to motivate you to make the best of your work sustainably. Lack of room to create your own meaningful goals in your work is therefore one of the most important reasons to start considering another job. You are the only one who can define what greatness means to you, so it is worth making an effort from time to time to explicitly formulate what would make you experience greatness.

> *You are the only one who can define what greatness means to you, so it is worth making an effort from time to time to explicitly formulate what would make you experience greatness.*

Throughout my career, I've formulated many goals, big and small—many of them so small that I don't even remember having them. They motivated me at that moment, though. I remember aspiring to do my first client meeting. I was nervous and overdressed; other people did the talking and I only observed, but I felt great afterward. I have spent parts of my career training myself to speak up in meetings. When I did so for the first time, I felt my heart pounding in my chest, but I increasingly discovered that people were actually grateful if I shared my thoughts with them. At one point in my career, I felt that I was too occupied with work, so I set myself the goal of not checking my e-mail during the evenings for at least a month. The good things about setting a target of doing this for a month are that it is feasible and that you have a clear moment when you will evaluate whether you will go back to what you had been doing or maybe carry on with the experiment for a longer period.

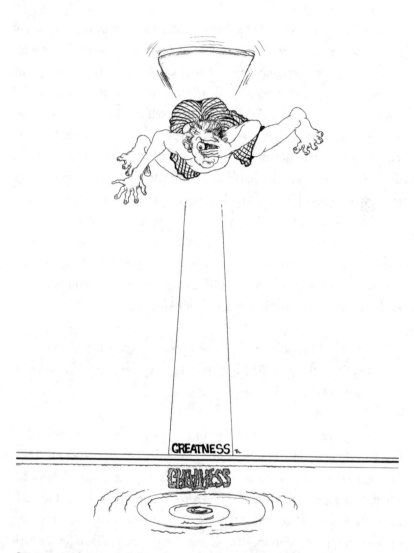

Greatness is what you define it to be; it includes both big and small milestones that help you to get up in the morning.

In this case, one month was sufficient to clarify some important things. I learned that I was afraid of not doing enough work, and I overcame that fear, so I could focus on work in a more relaxed way. That helped me to step back from time to time to evaluate whether I was still working on the right things in the right way and helped me to be much more efficient in the things I do. A common phrase among ambitious people is "Work hard, play hard." Though this sounds inspiring and heroic, I personally find more value in the phrase "Work smart, play smart." It is more important to work on the right things than to work on many things. Put in extra hours only when that really adds value, not just to show that you are working hard. Step back if your work allows you to, and you'll find that your mind is more focused and creative. You may suddenly feel ideas coming up that will help you leap forward. In my experience, productive creativity comes from finding the right cadence between doing things, connecting to people, and absorbing new information, on the one hand, and mentally relaxing from time to time, on the other hand. If you first stuff your mind with new impressions and then find the right moments to relax and reflect, your mind will unconsciously start putting things into place. This is why great ideas often come up while you are standing in the shower in the morning, cycling to work, or exercising. If you can create plenty of these moments of relaxation in your life, your subconscious will do a lot of the heavy lifting for you. You'll feel more energetic and productive as you do your work.

> *Productive creativity comes from finding the right cadence between doing things, connecting to people, and absorbing new information, on the one hand, and mentally relaxing from time to time, on the other hand.*

I've had various long-term aspirations, often based on meeting people I admired. In many cases, I had no idea at the time whether the aspirations were achievable for me. I've been lucky enough to achieve some of those aspirations faster than I ever expected. When I aspired to become a brand strategist, I found myself discussing brand strategy with the biggest advertisers about two years later. I remember a moment of cheer in the back of my head when I was discussing brand strategy with one of my clients, noticing they valued what I had to say about their brands. When I set that goal, I never expected that I would already have achieved it in two years' time.

Every time I achieve a long-term goal, I try to remember the moment when I formulated that goal. What kind of job was I doing back then? How did I assess my talents and skills at that moment? What were my aspirations and expectations? I mostly notice that I've underestimated myself in almost all stages of my career. The funny thing is that I underestimated how much time and effort it takes to build a career, yet I have become more successful than I expected to be. When I graduated from college, I expected that companies would welcome me with open arms and give me great work that I would quickly master, resulting in a smooth career path. Reality wasn't that smooth at all. I found that after graduation, you are just a starter again who has to build many professional skills. It took me a long time to find out how to best use my talents in my professional life and what kind of work inspired me most. It wasn't one moment of insight that made me find my direction, but a process of hard work and of trial and error. Yet I am now at a place in my career that did not enter my mind as something achievable in the first years of my working life.

Strangely enough, every time I have achieved a long-term goal, it was both a moment of celebration and a moment of small personal crisis. Achieving a goal that I didn't expect to achieve meant that I lost my sense of direction. At those moments, I basically had to redo my awareness exercise (Chapter 4) from the ground up: I redefined the skills that I had achieved, the talents that I had discovered, and which ones of those I enjoyed using most. I then reassessed how those skills and talents could be relevant for companies or for starting my own company. Based on that information, I had additional conversations with friends and colleagues, again often resulting in a change of job inside or outside the company, thereby creating room for development in a desired direction.

It is the combination of achieving multiple long- and short-term milestones that will create a ripple effect, resulting in moonshots. Long-term goals help you set the bar high enough so that you really aim for the moonshot. Short-term goals help you take the first steps toward getting there, and very often they create a surprising chain reaction by opening up new opportunities that you may not have seen before. Setting goals for yourself helps you acquire skills, and knowing that you have those skills will make you raise the bar for your next goals. The art of creating success and happiness in your career is a matter of balancing *perseverance* and *patience*. Perseverance is driven by the continuous urge to make the most out of what you have, while patience is driven by the appreciation of what you have. There are many people who have perseverance and many people who are patient, but there are very few people who can combine the two. People who are driven to succeed are likely to have some edge of dissatisfaction because they are not getting where they want to be. They keep raising their bars, but they fail to reward and appreciate themselves for where they already are. People who have the skill to be patient tend to be more appreciative of what they have and who they are, yet they sometimes lack the edge that would help them be even better. When they look back after many years, they may start wondering whether they should have made more of an effort and been more ambitious.

> *The art of creating success and happiness in your career is a matter of balancing* perseverance *and* patience.

Try to combine perseverance and patience at all times. Allow yourself to dream of big, aspirational things while setting achievable goals that will help you get there. Then commit to doing what is needed to make those goals happen. That will help you keep the perseverance to achieve the future that you aspire to. At the same time, look at what you have now: your health, your friends and family, your talents, and maybe the fact that you have some kind of income at all. See the big and small successes that you are building. None of them can be taken for granted. Match your expectations to what is realistic, and you'll feel more relaxed.

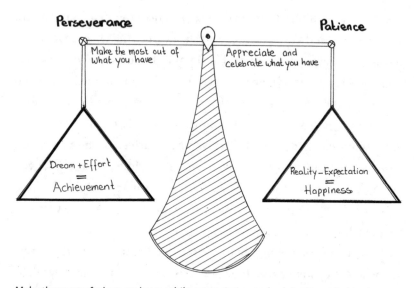

Make the most of what you have, while appreciating and celebrating what is given to you.

When are you successful? That is totally up to you, and your perspective on this matter most likely changes over time. Try not to compare yourself to others. You can use other people as a source of inspiration (and also for what *not* to do), but don't create a competition with others to evaluate whether you are successful or not. Everyone has a unique path for personal and professional development. People have different talents and get different opportunities. You are successful if you feel that you have used the talents and opportunities available to you in achieving milestones that you defined for yourself.

> *You can use other people as a source of inspiration, but don't create a competition with others to evaluate whether you are successful or not.*

There may be moments in both your private life and your career when you feel discouraged. Your new job may not be as nice as you expected; projects may go wrong; you may lose your job or have an annoying conflict with your manager. In your private life, you may experience illness, the loss of a loved one, or the breakup of a relationship. All of these have been true of me at some point in my career. There may be times when you feel that getting out of bed in the morning is a challenge, either mentally or physically. If that happens, take the time to accept the deepness of the valley, whatever it is. Allow yourself to feel sad about what has happened. If you think it will help, reach out to people who care about you and who may be able to help. This could be your friends and family, but it could also be someone at work who is more than just a colleague. Sometimes just the act of sharing what's on your mind can make a difference. Then once you start to see some light again, evaluate step by step what things give you positive energy, and focus on those. That may go better some days than others. Sometimes the act of getting out of bed and connecting with people is already greatness in itself.

Take care of yourself and the people around you at all times. If possible, don't make a fundamental decision concerning change until you feel that you can see things clearly. Sometimes a problem can look so big that it blurs your appreciation for all the things you have. If you make decisions based on that, you may end up throwing away something that is valuable to you. For instance, it is generally better to switch jobs because you know you can improve your situation than to run away from something because you don't like it. The diary of awesomeness that I mentioned in Chapter 4 can help you discover what things give you the most energy now. You can make those things the basis for your next goals. If you don't know where you are heading, you may walk straight into the next disappointment. Try to approach victory and loss in the same way: by being grateful for the experience. This way, you can never lose. Focus on what you need to do to get to a better situation than the one you are now in.

> *Try to approach victory and loss in the same way: by being grateful for the experience. This way, you can never lose.*

Learn to appreciate what you have while making the most of it, and you'll get the best possible combination of sustainable success and happiness. You decide what greatness means to you, and you are free to readjust your milestones at any moment of your career in any direction. If you look at it like that, you cannot go wrong. Build sustainable relations with people, both at work and in your private life; share your ideas and listen to theirs; build great work that is meaningful to all of you; and celebrate your successes together. Greatness is for everyone. Define your own greatness, and it will help you make the best of your work and your life, whatever your situation or position. I wish you all the best in your career, and I hope my experiences as shared in this book will help you achieve your aspirations. If you'd like to get more tips and tricks, you can visit my website (www.jorismerks.com). I'll be publishing videos and articles sharing experiences on how to help companies grow digital and build your career based on that. Thank you for taking the time to read; now go and enjoy the ride!

INDEX

ABOUT THE AUTHOR

Joris Merks-Benjaminsen is Head of Digital Transformation at Google in the Netherlands, helping top 100 companies embed digital thinking into their strategies. His fresh thinking won him prizes for Dialogue Marketer of the Year for 2012 and Best Marketing Literature of the Year for 2013 for his book about the integration of online and offline marketing. Joris was also nominated for Company Researcher of the Year and Cross Media Man of the Year for 2013. Joris's career has taken him from competitive sports to media and advertising, from research to brand management, and from cross media to digital marketing and innovation.